ISLAMOPHOBIA, RACE, AND GLOBAL POLITICS

ISLAMOPHOBIA, RACE, AND GLOBAL POLITICS

Updated Edition

Nazia Kazi

ROWMAN & LITTLEFIELD
Lanham • Boulder • New York • London

Published by Rowman & Littlefield
An imprint of The Rowman & Littlefield Publishing Group, Inc.
4501 Forbes Boulevard, Suite 200, Lanham, Maryland 20706
https://rowman.com

86-90 Paul Street, London EC2A 4NE

British Library Cataloguing in Publication Information Available

Library of Congress Cataloging-in-Publication Data
Names: Kazi, Nazia, 1982– author.
Title: Islamophobia, race, and global politics / Nazia Kazi.
Description: Updated Edition. | Lanham : Rowman & Littlefield, 2021. | Revised edition of the author's Islamophobia, race, and global politics [2019] | Includes bibliographical references and index.
Identifiers: LCCN 2021020669 (print) | LCCN 2021020670 (ebook) | ISBN 9781538157091 (cloth) | ISBN 9781538157107 (paperback) | ISBN 9781538157114 (epub)
Subjects: LCSH: Islamophobia—United States. | Moral panics—United States. | Muslims—United States—Social conditions.
Classification: LCC E184.M88 K39 2021 (print) | LCC E184.M88 (ebook) | DDC 305.6/97—dc23
LC record available at https://lccn.loc.gov/2021020669
LC ebook record available at https://lccn.loc.gov/2021020670

Dedicated to Hasan and Tasnim

CONTENTS

PREFACE

As I put this book together, I received word that the officer who murdered Philando Castile was cleared of all charges by a jury: a jury that had seen video footage of Castile's death, recorded by his girlfriend in the moments following the gunshots. A jury that had *also* seen Castile calmly, collectedly, tell the officer, "Just so you know, I have a legally registered firearm." The officer says, "Don't reach for it." Castile responds, "I'm not." The officer quickly shoots him dead in a scene that haunts me to this day.

To me, it doesn't matter one bit that Philando Castile was beloved in his community (which he most certainly was). That he memorized the allergies of the students he served in the lunchroom and, when they were short on cash, helped them pay for their lunches (which he did). It doesn't matter that Diamond Reynolds, his girlfriend, and her child sat in the car and witnessed his murder before being put in the back of a police van (which they did). Evidence of Castile's humanity and warmth is not at issue. What is at issue is that "officer-involved shootings" (as the media so passively calls them) of black people are so very normalized, so commonplace, that a jury can, in spite of incontrovertible evidence, acquit the officer.

Just as a jury decided no criminal charges should be brought in the death of Kenneth Chamberlain Sr., a man who was killed by police after accidentally pushing the button on his LifeAid medical alert device. An audio recording of the man's murder even revealed the officer using racial slurs against Chamberlain, who was tasered and then shot dead.

What place, you might ask, do the deaths of Chamberlain and Castile—or, for that matter, Tamir Rice, Sandra Bland, Eric Garner, Mike Brown, and Oscar Grant—have in a book on Islamophobia?

Quite simply, it is this: rage has fueled the writing of this book. The source of my rage is state-sanctioned violence, the backbone of white supremacy. As this book will show, it is white supremacy that has left more than a million Iraqis dead at the hands of US-imposed violence,[1] just as it was white supremacy that allowed Mexican Americans to be lynched in the American Southwest for "crimes" such as speaking Spanish.[2]

You might be surprised that a social science professor is openly claiming that *rage* has inspired her to write a book. Many believe that academia is a place for dispassionate, rational, impartial reasoning—that emotional reactions have no place in the study of human culture and society. But let me ask: What does one say about a society that *calmly* debates whether or not the *state* was in its rights to gun down Ramarley Graham, a child, in his own home?

I teach at a predominantly white institution where students are often utterly unfamiliar with America's violent racial past and present. There is an entrenched callousness on racial matters, a sense of "well, that's just how things are"—what Ian Haney López calls "commonsense racism."[3] Many students cling to a latent belief that America is racially unequal *not* because of egregious miscarriages of justice but because the groups on the margins are somehow undeniably responsible for being there.

Yet one semester, something surprising happened in one of my classes. I was showing my students, who are about eighteen to twenty years old, a film called *Harvest of Empire: A History of Latinos in America*.[4] This documentary asks why Latinos come to the United States—many of them illegally—and juxtaposes that question with the oft-obscured fact of US military intervention in the countries from which these migrants come. When the lights dim and the documentary voice-over begins, an inevitable glassy-eyed inattentiveness often sweeps across their faces. Yet one semester, the section began that described the years of support the United States provided the regime of the dictator Rafael Trujillo in the Dominican Republic. As the film documented the systematic tortures, executions, and rapes that were part of Trujillo's rule, I saw a student wipe a tear from her cheek, horrified at the violence perpetrated by a onetime US ally. I cursed my *own* callousness at exploring something this disturbing—the US role in destabilizing governments across Latin America for its own enrichment—so cavalierly, without considering the possibility that a student might have an emotional reaction, as well they *should*. After a decade of teaching college students, I've noticed something remarkable: once they begin to recognize that the knowledge they've taken for granted about power and race is incomplete, students exercise deep humility and care about matters of justice. This book is meant to allow such a reckoning.

I don't believe that the social sciences are a place to be detached, neutral, or calm—especially when matters of justice are involved. Instead, our study of race should allow for us to have deeply human reactions to the discoveries we make.

Now, a note on my methodology. Parts of this book contain ethnographic data. As an anthropologist, I have conducted several years of fieldwork with Muslim American organizations grappling with questions of Islamophobia, race, and power. This involved attending Islamic conventions, conferences, and meetups to draw conclusions about how members of these groups were handling the shifting realities for Muslims in the United States. I draw heavily from this ethnographic data. However, when I do so, it is with special care to protect my subjects' anonymity. To this end, names and other identifying information have been changed.

I'd like to urge you *not* to see the quotes and commentary from Muslim Americans in this text as representing Muslim Americans as a whole. In other words, a quote from Yaqub or Muhammad is simply that—a quote from one person. It is not a reflection of "the Muslim American community." Indeed, as you will see, it's not especially useful to talk about "Muslim Americans." This group is so radically diverse in their political leanings, their socioeconomic backgrounds, and their racial identities that the term hardly makes any sense. More importantly, Muslims in the United States have drastically different experiences of Islamophobia. Some bear the brunt of state-sponsored anti-Muslim action, such as deportations, special registration, or detention. Others experience Islamophobia in the form of workplace discrimination or suspicion from their neighbors.

No, I am not telling a story about what it is like to be Muslim in America, for there exists no such story. Instead, this book is part of a much larger dialogue about how racial difference functions, both within the United States and on the global stage.

ACKNOWLEDGMENTS

First, a sincere thanks to Sarah Stanton, Rolf Janke, and Kate Powers for bringing this project to fruition.

This book is written with gratitude to my sisters, Ruby and Safia, and with fierce love for my nieces. I'm also indebted to my parents for their encouragement, to Anuj Shrestha's endless patience and humor, and to Neesha Shah and Kasturi Sen for their unwavering friendship as I worked on the second edition. At the CUNY Graduate Center, Vincent Crapanzano, Jeff Maskovsky, and Dana-Ain Davis provided valuable mentorship and feedback. Deepa Kumar's thoughtfulness and attentiveness to my work and her commitment to justice are not to be forgotten. Thanks to Sarah Grey at Grey Editing and to Marlon MacAllister for their attention to this manuscript. Much gratitude to Sheena Sood for her keen insights and heartfelt encouragement and to Olivia Curran Webster for her intersectional analysis.

My colleagues at Stockton University have supported this project at every turn. Many thanks to the Sociology/Anthropology faculty, the School of Social and Behavioral Sciences, the Office of Research and Sponsored Programs, and my union, SFT2275.

To Erika Ferringo and Anthony Vigliano, I am humbled by your feedback, wisdom, and care, and lucky to count you among my friends.

To my chosen family in Philadelphia and New York, and to all who have inspired me to join the fight against racial capitalism, empire, and state-sanctioned violence, I am in awe of your capacity to fight. Your wisdom surpasses anything I could offer in these pages.

To the students who dare to think beyond the confines of the familiar, know that you have inspired me to write this book. I'm looking at you, Kaltoum Alibrahimi, Kiara Thame, Askhia Khawaja, Rawan Maarouf, Aleyah Hassan, Nudar Chowdhury, Julissa Juarez, Michael Mandes, Veronica Rowland, Mariah Fabel, Sarah Holt, and countless others.

1

INTRODUCTION

Troubling Islamophobia

On November 12, 2015, shoppers and worshippers ambled through Burj al-Barajneh, the bustling neighborhood near Beirut, Lebanon. Primarily a Lebanese Shi'a community, Burj al-Barajneh is also home to Palestinian, Lebanese Christian, and Kurdish populations, among others. That Thursday, the first explosion tore through a crowded area near a mosque. As chaos erupted and people rushed to help, a second bomb exploded, decimating a nearby bakery. Just minutes apart, these attacks claimed the lives of dozens and injured hundreds. ISIS (the common acronym for the Islamist group Islamic State of Iraq and the Levant, also known as Da'esh) infamously took credit for these suicide bombings. Then, only a day later, ISIS struck again, this time in the trendy north Paris neighborhood of Saint-Denis. That day's shootings and suicide bombings took more than a hundred lives, making it one of the deadliest attacks in France since World War II.

Facebook immediately offered Parisians a chance to mark themselves "safe" after the attacks, letting their loved ones know of their well-being by a quick tap of the screen. Within hours, a French-flag photo overlay was available to Facebook users, a way of indicating their grief and solidarity with the people of Paris and their opposition to ISIS. Social media became the channel for a global outcry of grief and support for the people of Paris. The Sydney Opera House displayed the colors of the French flag, too, as did City Hall in San Francisco. This international outpouring of support, media captivation, and outrage over the Paris attacks stood in stark contrast to a striking silence regarding the Beirut attacks. Many in the United States didn't even know that ISIS had carried out an attack in Beirut. In an article in the *Atlantic*, David Graham refers to this disparity as the "empathy gap": "where innocent deaths on one side are more deserving of mourning than innocent deaths on the other."[1] Americans could all too easily see themselves in the victims of the Paris attacks: ordinary Westerners at music venues and cafés.

Much like the 9/11 attacks,[2] the Paris attacks were obsessively covered on television. The news was saturated with images of mourners weeping over the loss of their loved ones, flowers laid down at memorial sites, and Parisians attempting to pick up the pieces after these devastating attacks. When the media focus on and sensationalize tragedies, the result is something called "compassionate narcissism." This refers to a *patriotic sympathy* for victims generated by media attention.[3] Compassionate narcissism is a nationalistic feeling that arises when we are bombarded with images of the suffering of certain victims. "Standing with Paris" thus became a type of compassionate narcissism: the victims of Paris deserved our empathy, solidarity, and support, as had the victims of 9/11. It became commonplace in the United States to mourn the white and Western victims of ISIS, neglecting the fact that most of ISIS's victims have been Muslim. In 2017, a deadly terror attack at a mosque in Sinai, Egypt, would go relatively uncovered in the mainstream Western media. Perhaps these 311 victims of terrorism were unremarkable because they were Muslim, Arab, and non-Western.

In the United States, at the time of the Paris attacks, presidential candidates were vying for their parties' nominations and offered condolences to the families of the victims. Donald Trump, then one of many candidates for the Republican nomination, suggested that the damage could have been minimized had more Parisians been armed with guns. After the Paris attacks, Trump's campaign adopted a decidedly anti-Muslim platform, calling for a database and increased surveillance of the Muslim population.[4] Trump was hardly an outlier in his policy proposals: his fellow Republican candidate Ben Carson similarly advocated for a ban on refugees from the Middle East.[5] Infamously, it was the Paris attacks that prompted Trump to challenge Democratic presidential hopeful Hillary Clinton to call the threat to the United States and

Western security "radical Islam" *explicitly*, which she refused to do. Candidates from both political parties, including Republicans Jeb Bush and Marco Rubio, voiced support for increasing surveillance of Muslim communities and greater government monitoring of domestic "threats." It was clear: the United States saw *itself* in Paris, and the nation's presidential hopefuls were hell-bent on ensuring that what had happened there didn't happen again *here*.

In the classroom, my students and I tried to make sense of the asymmetry of sympathy and coverage between Paris and Beirut. One student offered a suggestion.

> "Paris is a global city. Tourists visit it. There's great dining and nightlife there. It's . . . it's *modern*," said one of my students—we'll call him Kyle.
>
> "And Beirut?" I asked him.
>
> "Beirut is . . . well, it's not Paris," Kyle said, with an assured certainty even in the vagueness of his claim. I projected a map onto a screen in front of my students.
>
> "*Where* is Beirut?" I asked this room full of twenty-year-olds. None of them could locate it. A few knew it was in Lebanon. One knew that Lebanon had been rocked by a civil war in the not-too-distant past. Without knowing much at all about it, my students nevertheless believed with great assuredness that Beirut "isn't Paris."

Except, of course, that Beirut has more in common with Paris than many Americans might initially think. The coastal city is famous for its wild nightlife, its decidedly "liberal" social culture, and its vibrant cinema and coffee-shop culture. Beirut is known as fashion forward, and the city is peppered with well-reputed museums. So how did Kyle—a thoughtful, sensitive student—arrive at his conclusion that Beirut was, as he put it, "*not* Paris?"

Kyle's comments reveal much about American attitudes about self and Other, East and West, us and them. Such attitudes tell us less about how we imagine the world and more about how we, here in the United States, imagine *ourselves*. Kyle's words reflect the central argument the scholar Edward Said made in his book *Orientalism*: that the West has understood the Arab and Muslim world as its quintessential *Other*.[6] It is rendered exotic, irrational, and barbaric. In short, it is everything "we" imagine ourselves *not* to be.

So how do Americans come to make sense of the world beyond their own?

As we will see in the pages that follow, our understanding of the world around us is shaped as much by what is hidden or withheld as by what we *are* taught. (There's a reason our young people yawn through countless lessons about the Boston Tea Party but very few know about John Brown's willingness to go to the gallows for racial equality.) Here in the United States, our geographical imaginations all too often reflect what anthropologist Pem Buck calls "learned ignorance."[7] The theory of learned ignorance argues that the things we do *not* know aren't simply, accidentally left out of our education. Instead, it asks us to consider *how* we collectively develop intellectual blind spots. Without fail, my students exclaim how surprised they are to learn about parts of US history and politics that they were never taught. To dismiss these omissions as "just things we never learned" misses a big part of the picture. The gaping holes in our political and historical education reflect much larger, more deliberate processes.

Take, for instance, the way the legacy of Rosa Parks is commonly understood—or rather, misunderstood. The civil rights icon was committed to an aggressive anti-racist activism.[8] Her act of protest on a segregated Alabama bus wasn't because she was a tired seamstress heading home from work, refusing to give up her seat. Far from it; it was a well-planned act of civil disobedience orchestrated by anti-racist activists, committed to disrupting everyday life in order to bring about racial justice, even when it meant violating the law. Parks herself came from a family that had suffered immensely under the threat of Klan violence. Yet by the time her legacy made it to our history textbooks, it had been distilled, watered down, even erased. By the time they graduate from high school, most students in Middle America have a vague sense of Rosa Parks as a tired old lady who didn't want to give up her seat. What are the costs of knowing about her anti-war and anticapitalist views? Who decided her image should be one of a tired woman on a bus instead of an ardent admirer of the militant antiracism of Malcolm X? How would our understanding of America's racial history change if we knew it was driven by people like Parks, people who were willing to break laws and disrupt social harmony in order to challenge America's foundational white supremacy?

To anthropologists like myself, *social silences* (those things that are not commonly, appropriately, or widely discussed) are worthy of serious consideration. We can learn a lot about a society by studying what it leaves out of popular discourse. If, for instance, you stopped average Philadelphians on the street and asked them what significance the date May 13, 1985, holds for the city, you'd likely be met with many a blank stare. Yet the date is remarkable: it was the *only* time in US history that local law enforcement has ever carried out an aerial bombardment of a residential neighborhood. The attack, on a black activist community known as the MOVE organization,[9] left children dead and many bystanders homeless. It was an act of gross and deliberate negligence and racial violence perpetrated by city officials and law enforcement. After the bombing, rather than rushing to extinguish the flames and save lives, the police commissioner told firefighters to "let the fire burn."[10] (I recommended a film by that title to a student. He watched it, then caught me after class once to say, "Yo, I watched that movie. American history is *wild*. Too bad I never learned it.") This isn't an ancient story—it happened in my own lifetime. And it didn't happen "over there" (in a faraway country where Americans all too often *expect* such acts of state-sponsored barbarism). It happened just a short train ride from my own Philadelphia home. It's a moment that residents of that city block *do* remember with remarkable clarity, a day that had devastating effects.

What would it mean if the MOVE bombing *were* a part of middle school history lessons across the United States? How, then, might young Philadelphians regard the statue of Frank Rizzo, the police commissioner turned mayor who oversaw the bombing, a statue that stood for years in front of the Municipal Services building downtown, right across the street from City Hall?[11] (In fact, organizers who did know this history forced the city in 2017 to agree to move the statue to a new location.) How would they feel about the nature of law enforcement if they learned of the callous disregard for human life that the MOVE bombing illustrates, or how authority figures have long enacted what Bryan Stevenson calls "racial terror" on black and brown communities?[12]

Understanding learned ignorance allows us to accept that our worldview isn't shaped by objective facts, but through the *production* of facts that are taught to us in school, at home, in front of the television set, and in church. So, yes, there are very complex political reasons most Americans *don't know* about the vibrant urban culture of a city like Beirut. There are reasons most don't know about the deeply militarized nature of the MOVE bombing in West Philadelphia or about the radical activism of Rosa Parks. These reasons are not accidental; they are *systemic*. As we will see, long histories of decision making, economic inequality, and censorship led us here.

WHAT IS ISLAMOPHOBIA?

Today the term *Islamophobia* stands as an undeniable part of the American racial vocabulary. There are academic journals devoted to it. More and more colleges offer courses that deal explicitly with anti-Muslim sentiment. Muslim comedians Aziz Ansari and Kumail Nanjiani devoted two separate *Saturday Night Live* monologues to the topic in the aftermath of Trump's inauguration.

But as a term that has only recently become widely known in the United States, Islamophobia is all too often misunderstood, carelessly invoked, or too broadly applied. In the chapters that follow, we will see that Islamophobia isn't *simply* anti-Muslim sentiment. It isn't limited to acts of discrimination against women in headscarves or prejudice against Arabs. Instead, I ask in the pages to follow that we rethink anti-Muslim racism. In so doing, we can actually begin to better understand American race politics at large.

A several-hundred-page think tank report sits on my desk, the word *Islamophobia* splashed across the cover. Its pages include detailed documentation of acts of hostility toward Muslims: angry strangers pulling off women's headscarves on public transportation, mosques being vandalized, Muslim-owned restaurants finding racial slurs spray-painted across their storefronts, and strangers calling visibly Muslim pedestrians terrorists. It lists countless incidents of anti-Muslim graffiti; commonplace acts of violence against Arabs, Muslims, and South Asians; and threats made on the Internet. Certainly, such acts *are* a frequent and troubling feature of life for many US Muslims. Hassan, a seventy-year-old man, told me that when he goes to his suburban Michigan mosque, white teenage boys often come screeching around the corner, rolling down their windows and yelling phrases like "Allahu Akbar, ragheads!"

at worshippers. Nabeela, a woman in New Jersey who wears a hijab, says taunts such as "terrorist!" and "go back to your country!" are now abundant when she walks with her children to the local park, and have increased since the election of Donald Trump. I hear similar tales from my Muslim students, who navigate an intensely hostile campus environment in their day-to-day lives.

The think tank tome (it weighs just under a pound!) is replete with examples of everyday discrimination and harassment. Indeed, such incidents are commonplace. Yet the extensive report *never* mentions warfare. It doesn't include the sanctions passed by wealthy nations such as the United States that have kept countless Muslims from accessing basic necessities like food, school supplies, and medicine. It doesn't mention the menacing presence of military bases on foreign soil or unmanned drones that carry out strikes, killing Muslim civilians whose lost lives often don't even get tallied. It doesn't mention the totalitarian monarchs in Gulf countries who receive handy support from the United States even as they behead citizens and repress democratic uprisings.[13] Why don't *these* devastating realities count as Islamophobia?

We will see in this book that anti-Muslim slurs, taunts, and vandalism are the tip of a much larger iceberg. What lies below the surface includes a terror watch list kept by intelligence agencies that is growing exponentially, criminalizing Muslims and activists; a war machine whose budget is mammoth; a network of "experts" and "academics" who spew what passes for legitimate knowledge about the backwardness of Arabs and Muslims; and a media that skewers Muslims as antimodern or barbaric.[14]

Yet as the term *Islamophobia* gains acceptance in the lexicon of race studies, many have come to equate it with everyday insults and injuries against Muslims. All too often, the analysis stops there. Often ignored are the *political* practices that have rendered several Muslim-majority countries enemies in the eyes of Americans. This is a dangerous omission. This book, then, is not exactly about "Islamophobia." It will reflect on the institutional apparatuses that have singled out countless Muslims for detention, policing, and surveillance. It will also consider the banal mechanisms that render Muslims hypervisible—watched and investigated by curious readers, students, neighbors, and subway passengers. But this is not enough. We must also consider how each of these is related to the longstanding realities of white supremacy and US global domination. In so doing, we can begin to "trouble" the concept of Islamophobia. We will see why it's absolutely necessary to see Islamophobia not simply as individual acts of prejudice or bigotry, but as a cornerstone of an overarching system of white supremacy.

"LOOKING MUSLIM"

In Spike Lee's film *Inside Man*,[15] a hostage crisis erupts in a Manhattan bank. NYPD officers, detectives, and hostage negotiators descend on the city block. Suddenly, the bank robbers send a hostage, hooded and bound, out into the streets. He is surrounded by NYPD, their weapons drawn, as one cop exclaims, "Oh shit, it's an Arab! Is this a bomb?" (The hostage is wearing a turban.) The cop pushes the man down to his knees and pulls the turban off his head. Later, Vikram sits in a coffee shop with two black NYPD detectives, played by Denzel Washington and Chiwetel Ejiofor.

> "Where's my turban? I'm not talking to anybody without a turban. It's part of my religion, to cover my head in respect to God. I'm a Sikh."
> "Okay, we'll find your turban."
> "I'm not an Arab, by the way, like your cops called me outside."
> "Now, I don't think you heard that. There was a lot going on; you were probably disoriented. I didn't hear that."
> "I heard what I heard. I'll give you all the information you want. I just need my turban. It's part of my religion."
> "We'll get your turban. . . . We'll get an officer to come down. You can write a formal complaint. But for now, we got to deal with this situation."
> "First you beat me and now you want my help? . . . I'm fucking tired of this shit. What happened to my fucking civil rights? Why can't I go anywhere without being harassed? I get thrown out of a bank. I'm a hostage. I get harassed. I go to the airport. I can't go through security without a random selection. Fucking random my ass."

The scene captures a unique reality of the racial landscape of post-9/11 America. Specifically, it illustrates how even those who *aren't* Muslim have become targets of the Islamophobic landscape. Many observant Sikh men carry visible markers of their faith, including a turban and uncut hair. Though they are neither Muslim nor Arab, Sikhs have been swept up in the anti-Muslim furor. So deep is this perception that President Obama, when he visited India in 2012, canceled his visit to the Sikh Golden Temple, which requires visitors to cover their heads. Obama wanted to avoid the possibility of "appearing Muslim" in photographs.[16] In 2012, Wade Michael Page, an avowed white supremacist, committed a mass shooting at a Sikh gurdwara in Oak Creek, Wisconsin. Page murdered six worshippers and injured many others before killing himself. Would the massacre have taken place if brown-skinned people with beards and turbans were not seen as Muslim? In the eyes of a white supremacist like Page, did the difference even matter? For Sikhs who are singled out for "random" searches at airports and targeted in hate crimes and vandalism, repeatedly reminding people that they are "not Muslim" is a weak shield. In the United States, brown skin, a turban, a foreign-sounding name, and a black beard are enough to label one a Muslim—regardless of the facts. In 2012, a Hindu man, Sunando Sen, was killed after a woman pushed him in front of a subway train in what was understood to be an act of Islamophobia. For her, the fact that he was Hindu, not Muslim, hardly mattered.

The term *Islamophobia* is somewhat of a misnomer: it carries with it an assumption that it targets those who follow the religion of Islam—which is hardly the case. As Steven Salaita writes, Islamophobia "doesn't actually arise from the subject but squarely implicates the purveyor."[17] Islamophobia is in the eye of the beholder.

To those born and raised in the post-9/11 terror age, "Arab" is quite simply *equal* to "Muslim." Many of my students are surprised to learn that there are Arab Christians. The collapse of the Ottoman Empire brought an influx of Arab migrants to the United States in the early 1900s. Many of them were Christian. In fact, US maps are dotted with towns with names like Medina, Lebanon, and Palestine, so named because of this wave of migration. These immigrants, often labeled in the records as "Turks" or "Syrians," arrived in the United States and infused an undeniable Arab influence into American culture. Arab Christians, much like Sikhs and Hindus, are affected by Islamophobia in spite of the fact that they're not Muslim. Consider the murder of Lebanese Christian Khalid Jabara in 2016: his attacker, Stanley Majors, repeatedly called Jabara a "dirty Arab" and a "filthy Lebanese" before eventually killing him.[18] Jabara's murder further affirms Salaita's claim that "Arab Christians . . . are usually relegated into an Islamic identity in the discourse of many American racists, who often base their dislike (or fear) of Arabs on the misrepresentations of Islam pervasive in American popular culture."[19]

Consider, too, the experience of Latinx migrants in the United States and the increased militarization of the US-Mexico border. We might assume that xenophobia against Latin Americans has nothing to do with prejudice against Muslims. Yet let's look a little closer. In 2010, Arizona implemented one of the most draconian anti-immigrant laws in US history, SB1070. This law granted police the power to racially profile those they *suspect* of being undocumented. (You may note the irony of passing this law in a state with one of the largest Native American populations. A further irony? Not too long ago, Arizona was *part* of Mexico. Mexican Americans didn't cross the border—the border crossed them. They were residents of Arizona before there even *was* a United States.)

While America has long been preoccupied with "illegal" immigrants from Latin America, this anxiety intensified after 9/11. During this time, the very notion of "homeland security" gained momentum. It became easy for people in power to argue that our borders are weak. Increasing Border Patrol agents, border surveillance, and deportations thus became important priorities. Islamophobia played no small part in giving rise to a widespread assumption that America needs to be *secured*. This strangely overlapping fear of Muslims *and* Latinxs had thousands of Americans chanting "build a wall" at rallies in the 2016 presidential race. In 2016, conservative media outlets began spreading unverified rumors that ISIS was setting up terror cells in Mexico and across Latin America and that a weak border would render US citizens vulnerable not just to "illegal" Mexicans crossing the border, but also to Muslim terrorists. Again, we see Islamophobia's tentacles reaching beyond Muslims.

BARACK HUSSEIN OBAMA

Perhaps the most visible example of a non-Muslim being "accused" of being Muslim is Barack Obama himself. Obama's 2008 presidential campaign sparked a controversial public discussion about his religious identity. Many panicked Americans found themselves asking: Was Barack *Hussein* Obama a Muslim? In a presidential debate, a woman stood up to ask a question. "I can't trust Obama," she said to candidate John McCain and the scores of Americans who had tuned in to watch the debates. "I have read about him, and he's an Arab."

The implications were clear: *actually* being Muslim or Arab would easily disqualify Obama from the presidency—not by legal means, but by a "commonsense" social censure. The suspicion this woman had reserved for Obama was not hers alone. In fact, Donald Trump demanded that Obama produce his birth certificate, launching the infamous "Birther" movement that held that Obama was not an American and thus that his presidency was illegal. The ruckus revealed an unspoken understanding in the American imagination that Muslims have no business in the Oval Office. Consider the Ohio radio host who repeatedly mocked Obama's middle name, Hussein, while encouraging listeners to vote for McCain.[20] Obama's defenders were quick to point out that he is not Muslim, leaving the underlying Islamophobia unaddressed. Surprisingly, it was a Republican, Colin Powell, who brought it up. Appearing on *Meet the Press*, the former Secretary of State said,

> I'm also troubled by . . . what members of the party say, and it is permitted to be said. Such things as, "We know that Mr. Obama is a Muslim." Well, the correct answer is, he's not a Muslim. He's a Christian. He's always been a Christian. But the *really* right answer is—what if he is? Is there something wrong with being a Muslim in this country? . . . Is there something wrong with some seven-year-old Muslim American kid believing that he or she could be president?[21]

It didn't matter that Obama had distanced himself from Muslims during his presidential campaigns. His team even asked women in hijab to step out of the camera frame at a Detroit rally.[22] It didn't matter that Obama very visibly attended Christian church regularly or that he vocally aligned himself with Christian values. What did matter in this case were his foreign-sounding name, the color of his skin, and the fact that he hadn't grown up entirely in the West. Despite repeated assurances to the contrary, Obama *was read as* Muslim—and was thus subject to the workings of a virulent brand of anti-Muslim hysteria. This racial anxiety reveals what Junaid Rana calls the "Islamic peril."[23]

MUSLIM DIVERSITY

Even among actual Muslims, experiences of Islamophobia vary widely. Muslim Americans are far from homogenous; in fact, the term *Muslim American* often hides more than it reveals. As a catch-all category, it glosses over the range of experiences of being Muslim in the United States. While a working-class Bangladeshi neighborhood in the Jackson Heights section of Queens, New York, might be largely Muslim, it has little in common with an affluent Muslim community in, say, suburban Chicagoland. Arab American neighborhoods in Michigan don't much resemble the Somali communities that have set down roots in Minnesota. And worshippers at the predominantly African American Masjid Al-Taqwa mosque in Brooklyn look nothing like those at the Muslim Community Association mosque in Silicon Valley, where a large number of South Asian and Arab American Muslim professionals work in tech and finance. What we might be tempted to call "Muslim" neighborhoods in the United States are often not truly Muslim neighborhoods: they are ethnic enclaves. The people we call "Muslim Americans" are as stratified, segregated, and divided as the American population itself is, especially along lines of race and class.

The stories of Muslims arriving on these shores are equally varied.

The transatlantic slave trade brought Muslims from Africa, many of whom continued to practice Islam secretly despite violent forced conversions to Christianity.[24] Other enslaved Africans who became Christian held on to Islamic traditions that have had lasting impacts on African American culture. Yarrow Mamout, who lived in Washington, DC's Georgetown neighborhood in the early nineteenth century, was one of the few known enslaved people to resist conversion.[25] After being manumitted (released from slavery by his legal "owner"), Mamout became a visible and vocal practicing Muslim, widely known in his community. Today a portrait of him painted by Charles Willson Peale hangs in the Philadelphia Museum of Art.

The collapse of the Ottoman Empire in the early 1900s brought many West Asian Muslims to the United States.[26] This period also saw an influx of Yugoslavian and Albanian Muslims. Decades later, US immigration policy during and following the Cold War recruited droves of Muslim professionals, including scientists, engineers, and physicians from South Asia. (I certainly would not live here were it not for this wave of migration.) These professionals often sponsored relatives from their native countries, such as India and Pakistan, to emigrate, resulting in a two-tiered Asian immigrant population through what is often called chain migration. In the late twentieth century, South Asian Muslims from the West Indies (Guyana, Trinidad, Jamaica) also migrated to the United States. Following the Iranian revolution in 1979, there was a surge in the Irani Muslim population in America, and subsequently a marked rise in the proportion of Shi'ite Muslims. In recent decades, Muslim refugees from Bosnia and Somalia led to a growth in the presence of Muslims in small rural towns across the country.[27] Recently, the rise in Latinx converts to Islam has also captured the attention of the mainstream media.[28]

This brief overview ought to illuminate the fact that Islam in America is no monolith. The group we call "Muslim Americans" includes all elements of the racial and socioeconomic spectrum. It includes religiously observant, pious Muslims as well as those who only loosely identify with the faith tradition. It includes those who came over centuries ago and relatively recent arrivals. As Tariq Ali writes, "The world of Islam has not been monolithic for over a thousand years. The social and cultural differences between Senegalese, Chinese, Indonesian, Arab and South Asian Muslims are far greater than the similarities they share with non-Muslim members of the same nationality."[29] Yet Americans imagine a "Muslim world" that simply doesn't exist, flattening crucial differences along historical, racial, and cultural lines.

When scholar Reza Aslan appeared on CNN in 2014, Alisyn Camerota and Don Lemon bombarded him with uninformed questions about whether Islam promotes violence and whether sexism is inherent to Islam. In spite of Aslan's repeated reminders that Islam has over 1.5 billion followers, that Muslim women have been heads of state in several Muslim-majority countries, and that it's foolish to compare countries like Turkey and Bangladesh to Iran or Saudi Arabia, their questions about "the Muslim world" continued. Aslan retorted, "These kinds of conversations that we're having are not really being had in any legitimate kind of way. We're not talking about women in the Muslim world. We're using two or three examples to justify a generalization. That's actually the definition of bigotry."

Camerota replied, "So you don't think the justice system in Muslim countries . . . is somehow more primitive or subjugates women more than in other, Western countries?"

Reaching the end of his rope, Aslan snapped, "Did you hear what you just said? You said 'Muslim countries'. . . . To say 'Muslim countries' as though Indonesia and Pakistan are the same, as though somehow what is happening in the most extreme form of these repressive countries, is the same as what's happening in every other country, is frankly—and I use this word seriously—*stupid*, so let's stop doing that."

I quote this exchange at length because it shows how, all too often, "Islam" and "Muslims" are discussed as if these categories have any analytic unity. This is one of the shallow assumptions of Islamophobia: that there is such a thing as "the Muslim world." There isn't.

HOW DO WE TROUBLE ISLAMOPHOBIA?

This title of this chapter is "Troubling Islamophobia." It serves as a reminder that we ought to be nuanced when we use the word, perhaps even skeptical of overusing it. *Islamophobia* is certainly a useful term for documenting incidents of discrimination. (In my research, for example, I heard countless stories about Muslim travelers being routinely singled out for pat-downs, secondary screenings, and hostile remarks by passengers and flight crews.) But when we focus on this at the expense of systemic anti-Muslim practices, we miss a crucial part of the picture. We miss the ways Islamophobia *isn't* simply about the bigoted views of an ignorant guy on the subway platform. At its core, as we will discover in the chapters that follow, Islamophobia is about policies and practices that are commonplace and, more often than not, funded by our tax dollars. If we can move away from understanding Islamophobia as a matter of individual prejudice and toward understanding it as a fixture of our political and economic systems, we can begin to make better sense of racism in the United States.

In the days following the November 8, 2016, presidential election, liberals expressed alarm at Donald Trump's campaign promise to create a database of Muslims if he were to be elected. Many non-Muslim allies expressed passionate opposition to any such measures and vowed that if such a registry were built, they would be the first to sign up, rendering it ineffective. Organizers who had worked tirelessly for years against the National Security Entry-Exit Registration System (NSEERS, commonly known as Special Registration), which was established shortly after 9/11 and remained intact well into the Obama administration with no massive protests, were befuddled. Why the sudden popular opposition to a Muslim registry now? Those targeted by NSEERS had been singled out because of their origins in Muslim-majority countries: Special Registration profiled Muslim migrants on the basis of religion, which led civil liberties organizations like the ACLU to label it Islamophobic. Yet millions of American-born, US citizen Muslims were unaffected by—and many of them blissfully unaware of—the ravaging effects of Special Registration.

Why, then, were so many liberal Americans so vocally opposed to a Muslim registry system when it cropped up in the wake of the Trump election? Why hadn't they expressed such opposition to the *existing* Muslim registry? Was it because, in the immediate aftermath of 9/11, fear and anxiety were so widespread that people were ready to throw out their political principles? Was it because, rather than targeting *all* Muslims, NSEERS mainly targeted working-class, immigrant Muslims? And if so, what does it mean that a large liberal population will stand with Muslims—but only *certain* Muslims and at *certain* times?

The case of Special Registration shows the need to further trouble Islamophobia. We must be careful to not get caught up in assumptions about Muslims as a group or assume they are uniform in the ways they experience anti-Muslim sentiment. Instead, we ought to be diligent, deliberate, and thoughtful in acknowledging how socioeconomic class, immigration status, gender, and race impact the ways Islamophobia works. This book is an attempt to demystify Islamophobia, to get us past a simplistic framework that tells us that Islamophobia exists because there are ignorant, bigoted, anti-Muslim Americans out there.

This is a difficult shift to make. It forces us to realize that working against racism will not be as simple as signing up "in solidarity" against a racist registration system or "resisting" a single political figure. You might recall that many Americans in late 2016 felt that wearing a safety pin on one's shirt would indicate support for people of color. This symbol of solidarity with minorities was modeled off people in Britain who had worn safety pins to show support for immigrants in the midst of the xenophobic Brexit debacle. But safety-pin solidarity is laughable in the face of intensifying racist violence. Many people of color found the safety pin to be a silent, even hollow, gesture or an admission of "white guilt." Critics thought it came at a time when white allies need to rally hard against racism, to move beyond symbols to tangible action.

A principled antiracism will require sober reflection on propaganda, politics, and the world around us. It will require critical thinking and alliance building with those who are *most* marginalized among us. In the case of Islamophobia, it will force us to look past the Muslim voices that make it to the mainstream (the ones who speak about Islamophobia on news shows or in comedy routines) and listen instead to voices that are all too often suppressed, silenced, or rendered illegitimate. Not until this is widely understood can Islamophobia—or, truly, *any* form of racism—begin to crumble.

2

THE VISUAL POLITICS OF RACISM AND ISLAMOPHOBIA

In late January 2017, crowds of protestors descended upon airports across the United States. They held signs that read "Refugees Are Welcome Here" and "First they came for the Muslims, and we said, 'Hell No!'" These protestors—thousands of them—were rallying against President Donald Trump's executive order to ban Muslims from a set of predetermined Muslim-majority countries from entering the country. While the Trump administration claimed that this was an antiterror measure, protestors felt that it was an instance of racial profiling, one that rested on an assumption that refugees and migrants from places like Syria or Iran inherently pose a "terrorist threat."

EXTREME VETTING

The travel ban came as no surprise. Indeed, it fulfilled one of Trump's campaign promises: "a total and complete shutdown of Muslims entering the United States until our country's representatives can figure out what is going on." (This statement would vanish from his campaign website shortly after Trump and his team started facing questions from the press.[1]) Trump made the unsubstantiated claim that terrorists would sneak into the United States by exploiting its refugee resettlement policy. For many Americans, Trump's claim awakened fears of a terrorist threat lurking among immigrants from the Middle East.

Trump used terms like *extreme vetting* to describe a related proposal to increase scrutiny on migrants. Such language suggested that existing inspections and protocols were too lax and vulnerable to manipulation by dangerous terrorists.

Immigration policy experts were quick to point out that refugee resettlement programs in the United States *already* vet migrants with extreme scrutiny. "Whoever wrote this order is evidently not aware that these screenings, procedures, and questions already exist," wrote Natasha Hall, a former immigration officer.[2] She describes intensive interviews that have long been part of US immigration procedures, well before Trump was elected. Many refugees have burst into tears or given up entirely on hopes of resettling in the United States due to the rigor and trauma of screening procedures alone.

The "Muslim ban" suffered a blow when a Washington judge issued a restraining order against it. A revised travel ban, referred to as "Muslim ban 2.0," was similarly blocked, with one judge writing that it "drips with religious intolerance, animus, and discrimination." With these blocks in place, the administration turned to the Supreme Court. In an initial hearing, the Supreme Court upheld a modified version of the travel ban, dashing the hopes of many activists and protestors. Trump responded by further modifying the ban, producing a third iteration that included North Korea and Venezuela in an attempt to make it seem less overtly anti-Muslim. This version too was blocked by a federal judge, but ultimately it was upheld by the Supreme Court late in 2017. In April 2018, the Supreme Court began hearing oral arguments regarding the travel ban. In its final decision, the Court would rule in favor of Trump's "Muslim ban."

Many Americans thought the travel ban was good common sense. After all, it *was* people who called themselves Muslims who had attacked the Pentagon and Twin Towers. It was Muslims who had carried out the mass shooting in San Bernardino. And in Europe, it was Muslims who carried out the 2015 Paris attacks and ISIS that took responsibility for the 2017 attacks in London, Manchester, and Barcelona. The notion that Muslims should be disproportionately profiled and policed is not a product of Trump but has been a fixture in American political discourse. Michelle Malkin's book *In Defense of Internment* argues that racial profiling makes good sense. She justifies the internment of Japanese Americans during World War II and the racial profiling of Arabs and Muslims. Hardly a fringe opinion, Malkin's book made the *New York Times* bestseller list. Geraldo Rivera agreed that though racially profiling Muslims was "degrading," it was, given the need to secure America, perfectly reasonable.[3]

Given the recent history of terrorism, profiling Muslims seems, quite simply, like "common sense."[4] But why, we might ask, hasn't the 2016 attack by a white nationalist who murdered six worshippers at a Montreal mosque become emblazoned in North American memory as a devastating terrorist incident? Why didn't the October 2017 attempted bombing of a North Carolina airport by Michael Estes spark a media maelstrom, generating conversations about terrorism and airport security? What about the case of Portland man Jeremy Joseph Christian who yelled racist slurs and ultimately killed two white men who came to the defense of the Muslim woman targeted in his rant? Does *this* count as terrorism? What of the Hindu man shot to death in Olathe, Kansas, because his assailant, Adam Purinton, assumed he was a Muslim man from Iran? Was Richard Collins III, a black college student who was stabbed and killed by a white supremacist, Sean Urbanski, a victim of terrorism? Did carrying out a bloody massacre at a Sikh temple in Wisconsin make Wade Michael Page a terrorist? Each of these incidents was politically motivated violence against civilians: the very definition of terrorism.

The case of Christian terrorist Robert Doggart remained strikingly absent from mainstream media and politicians' pontifications. A 2014 congressional candidate, Doggart stockpiled weapons and plotted to massacre Muslims in 2017 in upstate New York in what he called a holy war. At his sentencing hearing, Judge Curtis Collier said, "You are not a monster. In many respects, you lived a life of honor."[5] Most would also be hard-pressed to recall the actions of Larry McQuilliams, who, inspired by a racist religious ideology, rained bullets on the police station, federal courthouse, and Mexican consulate in Austin, Texas. And when, in 2010, eight Christian white supremacists were arrested in Michigan for attempting to overthrow the US government, their case garnered scant media attention. White supremacist terrorism is all but invisible in the American social imaginary.

In 2017, classified documents from the FBI revealed a remarkable infiltration of white supremacists and militia extremists into US law enforcement.[6] The FBI memo spoke of "ghost skins," white supremacists who hide their racist beliefs in order to blend into mainstream society and propagate their views within law enforcement agencies, encouraged by skinheads. Case in point: in 2016, photos circulated on the internet of a Philadelphia police officer with clearly visible Nazi tattoos policing a protest, prompting outrage from social justice advocates. (Ultimately, he was found to be within his rights: it's perfectly permissible for a police officer to have a Nazi tattoo.)

What does our collective common sense have to say about all that?

THE SOUND OF THE DOG WHISTLE

That *terrorism* has become synonymous in the public imagination with *Muslim* violence is now a well-documented fact. It's no wonder the public makes this connection; acts of terrorism receive significantly more media coverage when the perpetrator is a Muslim.[7] A racialized word, *terrorism* works as a kind of racial dog whistle. *Dog whistle politics*, also called *muted racism*,[8] refers to the ways language that seems to be race-neutral is actually deeply racially charged. Dog whistling explains how policymakers speak of "inner-city gun violence" when they are actually talking about black people, or how "illegal immigrants" is a code word for Latin Americans. Indeed, our language is filled with such code words: the "girl next door" and "all-American boy" are invariably white, while "single inner-city moms" and "violent fundamentalists" signal certain populations of color. Our language is replete with ways to talk about race without ever actually mentioning it.

Dog whistling has been a crucial part of the US racial landscape ever since the civil rights movement forced antidiscrimination laws to be enacted and Jim Crow segregation to be dismantled. But in this new legal landscape, white supremacy didn't collapse. Far from it. The civil rights movement of the 1950s and 1960s didn't mark the end of racism, white supremacy, or racial inequality, but the birth of a new *type* of racism. Other mechanisms took the place of those that used to function to preserve white supremacy. In his book *Dog Whistle Politics: How Coded Racial Appeals Have Reinvented Racism and Wrecked the Middle Class*, Ian Haney López explains how Ronald Reagan was able to talk about black women by obliquely referring to welfare queens who bought T-bone steaks with their food stamps. In so doing, Reagan (as well as Bill Clinton, years later) propagated a *false* association of welfare with single, inner-city black women without ever overtly mentioning "race" or "black people." In our current post–civil rights age, when it is improper to be *overtly* racist, an intricate network of *covert* mechanisms keeps the longstanding racist order intact. Over half a century after the heyday of Martin Luther King Jr. and Rosa Parks, our schools remain deeply segregated, the wealth gap between white and black households remains staggering, and black Americans are arrested and incarcerated at an alarming and disproportionate rate when compared to whites.

In fact, the word *terrorism* itself serves as a dog whistle. "The term *terrorism* is never used to refer to the military violence of Western states, or the daily reality of gender-based violence, for example," Arun Kundnani reminds us, "both of which ought also to be labeled terrorism according the term's usual definition: violence against innocent civilians designed to advance a political cause."[9] To talk about terrorism in politics or the media is to talk about *Muslims*—without explicitly doing so. After the January protests at the Philadelphia airport, a protestor named Laura told me she came to the action because "it's obvious that Trump's using this language about keeping America safe from terrorism, but what he really means is keep Muslims and Arabs out." Many at the protests pointed out that the newly banned refugees themselves are often victims of terrorism. Many refugees are escaping the very same forces that the United States claims to be *fighting*. Yet much popular discourse conflates *migrant*, *refugee*, and *terrorist*. In the face of one of the largest migrant crises in recent history, refugees are regarded as unwanted, dangerous, or simply *not our problem.*

Of course, the latter assertion—that the United States doesn't "owe" migrants or refugees anything—couldn't be further from the truth. Many liberals argue that America ought to welcome migrants and refugees because, quite simply, it's the right thing to do. They claim that America is a nation built and made beautiful through a principled commitment to welcoming those fleeing persecution and threat. They refer to the Emma Lazarus poem displayed at Ellis Island: "Give me your tired, your poor / Your huddled masses yearning to breathe free."[10] We'll call this the dominant liberal narrative of inclusion. It tells us that migrants come here in search of a better life, and that welcoming them is the right thing to do.

THE CONDITIONS THAT CREATE MIGRATION

But why do migrants seek a better life here? What are the economic, political, and environmental *conditions* that lead migrants (many of them refugees) to seek a better life? And why does the United States hold the promise of that "better life" to begin with? The progressive notion that the United States ought to welcome immigrants because we are a merciful nation isn't just simplistic. It's false. The truth is that global superpowers *do* owe migrants and refugees a great deal. When we consider the United States' role in destabilizing, weakening, and impoverishing many of the regions from which immigrants come, the discussion about migration takes on an entirely new significance.

Take, for instance, the example of the robust Somali Muslim community in Minnesota. On the surface, it seems to be the perfect embodiment of the dominant liberal narrative. One of the largest Somali communities in the United States, Minnesotan Somali Muslims undoubtedly fled a country in Africa ravaged by war, poverty, and instability. In comparison, life in Minnesota seems vastly improved. The liberal narrative would suggest that the incorporation of Somalis in Minnesota is an example of American openness, its ability to welcome these tired, huddled masses.

Yet this script misses something critical: the deeply troubling political relationship between the US military and Somalia.[11] Geographically, Somalia has been of strategic interest to the United States. It became one of many countries in the so-called Third World where the United States and Soviet Union struggled for dominance during the Cold War. Often left out of our social studies textbooks, the fact is that the United States had a long history of backing dictators during the Cold War years—for instance, Siad Barre in Somalia, who was known to carry out horrific torture and imprison people who protested his rule, all with ample support from the United States. After the Cold War competition between the Soviet Union and the United States dissipated, the United States became interested in Somalia for its oil reserves.

In the early 1990s, the United States waged a vast military campaign in Somalia. This effort was advertised to the American public as "humanitarian," meant to alleviate hunger, remove corrupt warlords, and bring much-needed assistance to the poor and violence-plagued nation. Yet American soldiers were heard uttering the slogan "The only good

Somali is a dead Somali." During a 1993 massacre in Mogadishu, Somali civilians (including children) were targets for US troops. It's critical to note that the military effort in Somalia received support from both liberals and conservatives, including presidents George H. W. Bush and Bill Clinton.

Persistent US military intervention left Somalia in the throes of dwindling life expectancy, skyrocketing infant mortality, and rampant warfare. And this is just a *partial* history of US destabilization of Somalia. For instance, it was recently reported that the United States was operating a secret prison in Mogadishu.[12] At the time of this writing, Mogadishu had been rocked by a terror attack that killed hundreds, after the Trump administration increased its military action against a group called Al-Shabab. Somalia has reached a state of deep economic and political crisis. Famine and civil war have devastated the population. Michael Watts refers to the entrenched poverty and famine of African economies like Somalia's as "silent violence."[13] Knowing this history, the naïve claims to welcome Somalis out of a sense of mercy or generosity seem simplistic. Instead, a far more sinister reality surfaces: the United States itself is responsible for the plight—and flight—of Somalis. This isn't a matter of mercy, inclusion, or being a "land of immigrants." It's a matter of complicity.

THE MUSLIM BAN AND THE "GROUND ZERO MOSQUE"

The protests against the travel ban were energetic, angry, and fearful. They drew huge swaths of people from Jewish, LGBTQ, black and Latinx communities, as well as white allies. It reminded me of the protest energy years before at Ground Zero in Manhattan in 2010, when controversy had erupted around an attempt to build an Islamic community center in Lower Manhattan that would include space for prayer, athletics, childcare, and more. When the proposed Islamic center (or the "Ground Zero Mosque," as it came to be known) caught the attention of such prominent anti-Muslim spokespeople as Pamela Geller and Robert Spencer (founders of the group Stop Islamization of America), it led to much public debate, concern, and outcry. The controversy spread well beyond New York City, with even former Republican vice-presidential nominee Sarah Palin chiming in to ask "peace-seeking Muslims" to abandon plans to build the center.[14] Conservative Newt Gingrich called it "an assertion of Islamist triumphalism,"[15] while liberal Democrat Howard Dean told a radio station that building it would be "a real affront to people who lost their lives" on 9/11.[16] New Yorkers chimed in. Protests were held at the site, both in ferocious opposition to the plans and in support of Muslims' right to worship and convene.

On a strictly *legal* basis, there was no question that Muslims were absolutely within their rights to build the center. Instead, the public debate focused more closely on whether it was appropriate, insensitive, or proper for Muslims to build the center. The Muslim identity of the small number of 9/11 hijackers extended to the rest of the US Muslim population, to millions of people who had nothing whatsoever to do with the attacks. The debate about the Islamic center raged even *within* the Muslim community. On an episode of *Democracy Now!* professors Tariq Ramadan and Moustafa Bayoumi debated the issue. While they both agreed that the planners had the *right* to build the community center, Ramadan argued that they should cancel the project. "We have to think about the symbol," he said. "Muslims should think about not being instrumentalized in the whole process by political forces, but understand the collective *sensitivity*." I was doing fieldwork at the time and sat down to coffee with one of my fieldwork contacts, Samina. She said something very similar to what Ramadan had said:

> I disagree with people who are saying Muslims can't build a mosque near Ground Zero. That's straight-up Islamophobic. But there are all these protests happening there, and people on both sides are show-ing up. I feel like maybe I should go, but I don't know. I wear a hijab. I feel bad about what happened, the people who lost their lives there. I don't know if Americans are ready for Muslims to show up at these protests.

Several years later, I would hear similar reservations from Muslim Americans who were hesitant to attend the airport protests. After the Trump administration announced the executive order, Aminah, an American-born Muslim and college senior, told me she had wanted to go to the Philadelphia airport protests. "My parents begged me not to," she said with disappointment. Aminah obediently listened to her par-ents' pleas. "They think it's a bad idea to attend. That it will draw negative attention to me. They just keep telling me to focus on my schoolwork and not worry so much about politics." Aminah wasn't the only one. Many Muslims I spoke with felt that these pro-Muslim protest spaces weren't appropriate for them. While they supported the protests ideologically and politically, they felt uneasy being there and worried it would mark them culturally, racially, and politically. The majority of New York Muslims weren't actively involved with the protests around the Islamic center, just as the vast majority of US Muslims weren't present at the airport protests in 2017.

This is true of most social movements. Protests that emerge in public spaces, such as the airport convergence or the Ground Zero protests, usually only convene a small portion of the concerned population. During the height of the civil rights era, most African Americans were *not* marching on Washington or through Selma; it was a small subset of African Americans who did. People's political loyalties are not easily measured by their participation in rallies, marches, or protests.

American Muslims face a dilemma. They must make careful calculations of risk, reward, danger, and visibility when deciding how and whether to engage politically. Those decisions—for instance, to avoid being "seen" at controversial protests, even those they fundamentally support—reveal something called *Muslim hypervisibility*.[17] Scholar Sunaina Marr Maira describes this as "anxiety about public protest in communities that had been in the crosshairs of the surveillance state for many years."[18] In most public protests in Philadelphia, for instance, there is usually a uniformed police officer closely recording the entire action, including close shots of the faces of protestors. For Muslims anxious about government surveillance, this is especially harrowing.

The "Ground Zero mosque" controversy illustrates the *collective* accountability invoked upon Muslims. They are asked to modify their decisions about where to worship and even where to protest, as though the acts of a handful of 9/11 hijackers have anything to do with them. This wouldn't be true for a group that wasn't marginalized: Does the general public find it insensitive for Catholics to run elementary schools, given that *some* priests have been found to commit pedophilia? Do people find it inappropriate for a white Christian church to exist near a women's health clinic, given the history of Christian assaults on medical facilities that provide abortions? Why must the victims of bigotry shoulder the burden of collective blame?

INSTITUTIONAL HYPERVISIBILITY

The ways Muslims in the United States have found themselves examined, scrutinized, and monitored are key to understanding Islamophobia. This Muslim hypervisibility exists on two distinct—but interconnected—levels. First, there's *institutional hypervisibility*. This refers to official, legally mandated, state-based practices of policing and surveillance. Institutional hypervisibility is implemented through government policy and law-enforcement actions.[19] Second, we can think about *sociocultural hypervisibility*: everyday curiosity, concern, and watchfulness.

After 9/11, debates about the institutional hypervisibility of Muslims entered the public sphere. Take, for instance, the passage of the USA PATRIOT Act. This piece of legislation was supported by both Democrats and Republicans (authored by George W. Bush's administration but renewed and extended by Barack Obama's). It made surveillance of Muslims the law of the land. The Patriot Act, as it came to be known, allowed wiretaps and searches *without* a demonstration of probable criminal conduct. It also gave federal agents the power to search private residences and workplaces secretly, with minimal oversight or legal approval. This provision that came to be known as "sneak and peek" allowed law enforcement to search private premises clandestinely without the occupant's knowledge, based solely on a vague notion of "suspiciousness."

Local law enforcement began acting on the assumption that the next major terrorist attack would come not from a foreign entity but from a domestic Muslim one.[20] In terrorism-prevention and policing circles, this came to be known as "homegrown terrorism." Because the would-be terrorist might be from among *us*, intelligence agencies and law enforcement needed tools to clearly sniff out and label the identifiable enemy. In 2011, it was revealed to the public that the NYPD had been systematically spying on Muslims. This surveillance took place not only in mosques (which the NYPD designated "terrorist organizations") but also in bookstores, college student groups, cafés, and restaurants. The NYPD established its Demographics Unit, inspired by Israeli tactics in the West Bank, trained by the CIA, and enabled by overturning legal provisions around privacy, discrimination, and the jurisdiction given to law enforcement.

The Demographics Unit collected information on Muslims that it claimed would prevent another terrorist attack. This included what news channels were being watched in Muslim-owned cafés, what people were wearing, whether Muslims were talking about politics at a particular bookstore, what languages were being spoken, even who was playing chess. In other words, every ostensible part of Muslim existence was rendered suspicious and thus monitored.[21] The Demographics Unit was a remarkable waste of New York City resources: it never detected a single terror plot. Later disbanded after coming under attack from Muslim advocacy groups, it echoed a failed plan of the Los Angeles Police Department in 2007 to map and monitor Muslims. The LAPD claimed that it would identify potentially radicalized individuals by mapping out where Pakistanis, Iranians, and Chechens lived. Neither the NYPD nor the LAPD plan investigated terrorism. They were simply profiling Muslims.

Intelligence agencies have also used a tactic called *preemptive prosecution*,[22] in which they use paid informants and *agents provocateurs* to incite Muslims to attempt or support terrorist acts they may otherwise not have committed. Once they're "busted," the discovery of these would-be terrorists is claimed as a victory in the war against terrorism. For instance, Craig Monteilh, an ex-con who served a prison sentence for financial crimes, confessed to accepting huge sums of money from the FBI to pose as a Muslim in Southern California and lure worshippers into plotting terror acts. (The Muslims he was trying to entrap found his behavior troubling. In an almost comical turn of events, they ended up reporting him to the very FBI that had placed him there in the first place.)

Surveillance of Muslims is hardly limited to the Patriot Act or recent law enforcement initiatives. Consider, for instance, Operation Boulder, a government program from the early 1970s that singled out Arab and Middle Eastern Americans for surveillance. Prompted by the 1972 attacks at the Munich Olympics, in which Palestinian members of a group called Black September killed several Israeli athletes, Operation Boulder was dubbed unconstitutional by the American Civil Liberties Union.[23] More recently, Republican representative Peter King argued that the state ought to monitor mosques, since "mosques are where the threat is coming from." As head of the House Homeland Security Committee in 2011, King conducted several hearings on the radicalization of

Muslims, ostensible witch hunts that showed clear anti-Muslim bias. (King has publicly worried that there are "too many mosques" in America and that almost *all* Muslim American leaders are "the enemy living among us."[24]) And as noted, in the 2016 election both major candidates called for increased surveillance of Muslims. The disproportionate focus on Muslims for surveillance, then, is not the product of any one political party or any specific politician. It seems, instead, to be a sine qua non of the US racial order.

SOCIOCULTURAL HYPERVISIBILITY

Muslim hypervisibility isn't limited to surveillance, policing, mapping, and monitoring. Unofficial mechanisms keep a watchful eye over Muslims too. When I was doing my research with members of Muslim American organizations, I sat down with someone I'll call Aadam, a regular attendee of Islamic conventions. He described the post-9/11 moment with remarkable clarity. "Qurans were sold out and backordered at bookstores after September 11," he said. "On college campuses, there were all of a sudden tons of students registering for classes about Islam, Muslims, or the Middle East. And every news show had some segment about Muslims, trying to explain who Muslims are. To an extent, it was like knowing Muslims—knowing Muslim *culture*—was a way to know why these terrible things happened." This is sociocultural hypervisibility—a general public concern, fascination, and curiosity about who Muslims are.

Columbia University professor Lila Abu-Lughod spoke about her own interactions with the media.

> The presenter from *NewsHour* first contacted me in October 2001 to see if I would be willing to provide some background for a segment on Women and Islam. I agreed to look at the questions she was going to pose to panelists. I found them hopelessly general. Do Muslim women believe X? Does Islam allow Z . . . ? I asked her if she would ask the same questions about Christianity or Judaism. I did not imagine she would call me back. But she did, twice. The first was with an idea for a segment on the meaning of Ramadan, which was in response to an American bombing during that time. The second was for a program on Muslim women in politics, following speeches by

Laura Bush and Cherie Blair, wife of then British Prime Minister. What is striking about these ideas for new programs is that there was a consistent resort to the cultural, as if knowing something about . . . Islam or the meaning of a religious ritual would help one understand the tragic attack [on 9/11]; how Afghanistan had come to be ruled by the Taliban; . . . what the history of American support for conservative Afghan fighters might have been; or why the caves and bunkers out of which Osama bin Laden was to be smoked "dead or alive," as President Bush announced on television, were paid for and built by the CIA.[25]

Abu Lughod's experience show us how the hypervisibility of *Islam*—Muslim culture, religious practices, or traditional attire—takes focus *off* political histories. While it might make more sense for us to explore the history and politics of Western nations' relationships to the "Muslim world," we instead end up asking about cultural and religious practices. Instead of asking about the secret sites the United States operates in Somalia, Americans are more likely to ask why many young Muslim women choose to wear a headscarf. Rather than inquiring about the history of British military intervention in Libya, the public would rather ask about the significance of the holy month of Ramadan. This is the trade-off made in public discourse. It has become commonplace to eschew discussions of politics and opt instead for curiosity about Muslim culture or religious practice. (We'll return to the question of "culture talk" in chapter 5.)

The everyday curiosity about Muslims and Islam has had very real ramifications. It means that US Muslims now have a watchful gaze cast over them by the news media, by suspicious neighbors, by academics, even by sympathetic Americans. There's a voyeuristic fascination, too, an obsession, with locating, viewing, and understanding the Muslim American subject. On the college campus where I teach, as on many campuses across the country, there's often a "hijab day"—a day for non-Muslim women to try on a hijab and "experience" what it is like to be a Muslim woman for a day. Such samplings don't occur with, for instance, the Jewish yarmulke or the Sikh turban or other religious markers; instead we see an *exceptional* fascination with Muslims in general, the hijab in particular.

The espial focus on Muslims ranges from such sympathetic curiosity to outright suspicion. In East Stroudsburg, Pennsylvania, in 2016, a customer panicked at a gas station, calling police after spotting a "suspicious package." A bomb squad arrived. The gas station and nearby day care were shut down in an emergency reaction to the discovery. The suspicious package? A box of cookies with some Arabic writing along the side, easily purchased on Amazon. (The box was also clearly labeled, in English, as "date-filled cookies.") We ought to pause here and ask: What does it mean that the script of a major world language—one used by Muslims, Christians, Jews, and spoken at airports, restaurants, schools—is seen as "suspicious"? What are the conditions that caused the individual to panic and call law enforcement? What are the ramifications for Sikhs, Arabs, and Muslims, or for people who speak Arabic, Farsi, or Urdu, who wear hijabs and burqas, of being *watched*?

In the years after 9/11, in New York City subway stations and on MTA trains, billboards screamed at passengers: "If you see something, say something." Unattended packages and behavior put New Yorkers on high alert. "There are 16 million eyes in the city," one subway poster read. "We're counting on all of them." Such reminders served as an informal recruitment mechanism: the public was thus drafted into service as mediators between law enforcement and potential terrorists. Ordinary people were called upon to do the work of policing, asked to look at their city through new eyes.

If you see something, say something is part of a larger campaign implemented by the Department of Homeland Security (DHS). These words appear on college campuses, on Amtrak trains, and at city bus stops across the country. DHS's website advises people on what might count as suspicious activity: "a window/door is open that is usually closed" is included on the list, as is "loitering without explanation." Photographing or filming buildings is also counted among the criteria for suspicion. The website makes clear that "race, ethnicity, or religious affiliation are not suspicious."[26] I once sat at a counter in a restaurant in Philadelphia, striking up a conversation with a man we'll call Jeff. His hobby is photography, so Jeff travels around North Philadelphia, where countless abandoned buildings and warehouses stand as a reminder of economic deindustrialization.[27] Jeff photographs graffiti, condemned buildings, hourly motels, and other signs of the rampant blight that plagues Philly. A six-foot-tall man with blue eyes, blond hair, tattoo sleeves, and an on-trend man-bun, Jeff loiters, photographs, and opens and closes doors and windows in North Philly, yet this hardly warrants calls to Homeland Security. Jeff, in other words, is *not* suspicious. Date-filled cookies in a box with Arabic script, though, are.

Those of us with common Muslim names can tell you firsthand about the hassle of airline travel. And this isn't just about getting stopped by airline officials or the TSA, though that's certainly a huge part of it. There's also widespread discomfort among the general public regarding Muslim airline passengers.[28] Terms like *flying while brown* or *flying while Muslim* are commonplace ways to refer to the racist profiling of Muslim airline passengers. For example, NPR analyst Juan Williams (who was subsequently fired for his remarks) appeared on *The O'Reilly Factor* and said, "Look, Bill, I'm not a bigot. You know the kind of books I've written about the civil rights movement in this country. But when I get on a plane, I got to tell you, if I see people who are in Muslim garb and I think, you know, they are identifying themselves first and foremost as Muslims, I get worried. I get nervous." It was a classic "I'm not racist, but . . . " statement that cast guilt over any Muslim-looking airline passenger.

The people I met while doing my research were fully aware of their hypervisibility. I was told time and again that Islamic conventions, conferences, and meetings were assumed to have "at least one spy" present. Another circulating rumor was that the FBI's official policy was to have "at least one spy at every Friday prayer in order to record the sermon." Others told me they took clicks or interference on phone calls as evidence that their phones had been tapped. "You know, they have files on all of us," I was told casually by many of my interlocutors. Once, when interviewing someone at an Islamic convention, I was told, "For all I know, *you* might even be a spy posing as a researcher." I often heard jokes about surveillance; after a phone call, someone might say something like, "Later, NSA," referring not-so-obliquely to the National Security Agency and its expansive web of surveillance mechanisms. For them, it's become an obvious, immutable feature of life in the terror age. And for many Americans, it's become part of a new common sense that Muslims *need* to be watched over. As likely terrorists or ISIS sympathizers, they are seen as deserving this watchful eye, guilty until proven innocent.

BLACK LIVES AND HYPERVISIBILITY

For those of us who study race, Muslim hypervisibility comes as no surprise. Indeed, people of color have always had to deal with the persistent fact of being watched. To be racialized is to *be* hypervisible.

Black communities have experienced deep hypervisibility, both sociocultural and institutional. Black people have richly documented the experience of being followed by sales staff in high-end stores and being singled out for "driving while black"—routine roadside harassment of black drivers by law enforcement. Or consider the bizarre case of Harvard University professor Henry Louis Gates Jr., who in 2009 was arrested for attempting to enter his own home. Gates, a resident of an elite Cambridge neighborhood, had just returned from out of town and found his door jammed shut. Attempting to open it, he caught the eye of a local witness, who called 911. The police arrived and arrested Gates for disorderly conduct. Many race scholars were quick to point out that Gates was, in a sense, "violating apartheid"[29]: a black professor at Harvard and resident of a predominantly white, upper-class neighborhood, Gates was already marked with suspicion. His crime was simply existing where he wasn't "supposed to be." Gates's ordeal epitomizes racial hypervisibility. The incident almost comically echoed a standup bit from comedian Dave Chappelle in which he jokes about why, as a black man, he's reluctant to call the police.

> Somebody broke into my house once, but I didn't want to call the police. Nope, nuh-uh. My house is too nice. They'd never believe I lived in it. They'd be like, "He's still here!" [bang] "Oh my god. Open and shut case, Johnson. I saw this once before when I was a rookie. Apparently this n***** broke into this house and hung pictures of his family everywhere. Well, let's sprinkle some crack on him and get out of here."[30]

On a more sinister level, the state has an enduring history of deep prying into black lives. Surveillance mechanisms have long rendered black communities visible to those in positions of power. Mass protests erupted in New York following the strangling of Eric Garner by NYPD officer Daniel Pantaleo, who placed Garner in an illegal chokehold. (Garner uttered his last words, "I can't breathe," eleven times before his death. No one was ever held accountable for this murder.) The protests against Garner's death were alarming enough to law enforcement that they assembled a vast surveillance apparatus to spy on the protestors. After this uprising, Black Lives Matter (BLM) activists were routinely targeted by NYPD surveillance,[31] their text messages and email conversations monitored by an extensive network of undercover officers who penetrated the group.

The infiltration and surveillance of BLM is eerily reminiscent of the covert, illegal practices of the Counter Intelligence Program, known as COINTELPRO. In J. Edgar Hoover's FBI, COINTELPRO spied on activist groups, including the Black Panther Party, anti-war organizations, environmentalist groups, and the Puerto Rican independence movement.[32] The extent of the FBI's illegal surveillance came to light after a group of activists burglarized a Media, Pennsylvania, FBI office in 1971, obtaining top-secret documents (in a tale packed with enough intrigue to warrant a Hollywood retelling). These memos revealed in plain terms the state's widespread suppression of political engagement, dissent, and activism. The FBI was keeping files—extensive ones—on anyone engaged in leftist political organizing.

Yet perhaps more interestingly, the FBI was also spying on black people—*any and all* black people. You didn't have to be an activist, a political dissident, or a communist. FBI agents were closely monitoring "African Americans wherever they went—in churches, in classrooms, on college campuses, in bars, in restaurants, in bookstores, in their places of employment, in stores, in any social setting, in their neighborhoods, and even at the front doors of their homes," writes Betty Medsger in *The Nation*.[33] Such activities weren't limited to the FBI; even the NYPD had, during the 1960s, a special "black desk" dedicated to investigating African Americans.[34] The state, it seems, had an innate hostility to people of color.

Visual politics are intricately woven in to the workings of race and power around the world. Managing the dividing line between the watched and the watchers has persistently been part and parcel of power dynamics. In other words, maintaining hierarchies and domination has often meant managing what the colonized subject could and couldn't *see*. The British, for instance, were even careful to ensure that colonized subjects didn't see aging or frail white men. Edward Said tells us:

When it became common practice during the nineteenth century for Britain to retire its administrators from India and elsewhere once they had reached the age of fifty-five, then a further refinement in Orientalism had been achieved: no Oriental was ever allowed to see a Westerner as he aged and degenerated, just as no Westerner needed ever to see himself, mirrored in the eyes of the subject race, as anything but a vigorous, rational, ever-alert young Raj.[35]

Thus, it should come as no surprise that the Trump administration announced in 2017 the launch of a new agency, Victims of Immigration Crime Engagement (VOICE).[36] VOICE, it was reported, would single out undocumented immigrants who committed crimes against Americans. Speaking in defense of VOICE, John F. Kelly (then of the DHS) said, "All crime is terrible, but these victims are unique—and too often ignored. These are casualties of crimes that should never have taken place because the people who victimized them oftentimes should not have been in the country in the first place."

The criminalization of immigrants has been a longstanding feature of American political discourse.[37] Consider the discussions of migrants we see in the mainstream news media:[38]

Once again, the streets of our country were taken over today by people who don't belong here. America's illegal aliens are becoming ever-bolder. March through our streets and demand your rights? Excuse me! You have no rights here.

Listen, I'm for open immigration, but when the immigrants come, they come with a culture of criminality. It's out of control.

We want the folks across the United States to know that we're standing with them to protect American lives, liberty, and property from the invasion of the illegal aliens.

All those hundreds of thousands that sneak into this country, they could be diseased.

It was in the context of this preexisting criminalization of immigrants that Donald Trump said during his presidential campaign, "When Mexico sends its people, they're not sending their best . . . They're sending people that have lots of problems, and they're bringing those problems with. They're bringing drugs, they're bringing crime. They're rapists."[39]

As such, immigrants have been rendered hypervisible through allegations of criminality. In fact, when John Kelly was DHS secretary in early 2017, he ordered Immigration and Customs Enforcement (ICE) officials to spread the narrative that portrayed immigrants as criminals and ICE raids as making the public safer.[40] They were asked to focus on "egregious" cases of criminals being apprehended, shining a spotlight on the most offensive criminal outliers found in immigration raids. Essentially, Kelly was asking ICE to dramatically exaggerate immigrant criminality.

VOICE and its overt xenophobia prompted many liberals to take a defensive stance. They have presented statistics and anecdotal evidence proving that immigrants *aren't* criminals. In opposition to VOICE, they offer stories of law-abiding, hardworking immigrants targeted by anti-immigrant sentiment. They argue that immigrants commit crimes at lower rates than nonimmigrants. For instance, three decades of census data show immigrant men as one-half to one-fifth as likely as US-born men to be incarcerated.[41] These are important statistics. Yet this defense misses the point: the debate *should* not be about comparing crime rates between populations, but about the significance of singling out undocumented immigrants who commit crimes. A response that attempts to prove that immigrants aren't criminals dodges the much tougher issue: that the state is playing a dangerous game of racist fear-mongering in its singling out of migrants.

Let us not forget that the Nazis created an Institute for Research on the Jewish Question—a bureau that singled out crimes committed by Jews—as part of *their* anti-Semitic project.[42] What's striking about the Institute for Research on the Jewish Question is not that it investigated Jewish criminality: its most important accomplishment was that it raised among the general public the very *question* of Jewish criminality to begin with. In sparking a debate on "Jewish criminality," such an institute succeeded in *creating* the very problem of the "Jewish criminal." Like claims today that immigrants are law abiding, claims that Jews were no more or less criminal than the general public missed the point altogether.

Whether or not anyone can prove that immigrants aren't lawbreakers, creating an agency like VOICE successfully creates an implicit association in the general public between *immigrant* and *criminal*. Let us consider how it is that criminalization dehumanizes people. In 2010, eyewitness video footage recorded the murder of a forty-two-year-old man, Anastasio Hernández-Rojas, an undocumented immigrant trying to cross the border from Mexico. Hernández-Rojas had been living in California on and off since he was a teenager. Several bystanders recorded the brutal beating, which left Hernández-Rojas with broken ribs and spinal damage. He died shortly thereafter of a heart attack. Most of these video recordings didn't reach the public; the Border Patrol confiscated them. Yet one bystander, Ashley Young, secretly held on to her video and later mailed it to authorities, leading to a PBS documentary about the grisly murder.[43] This led to public outcry about brutality among Border Patrol agents. The footage is not for the faint of heart: Anastasio is heard yelling *"Ayudame!"* (Help me!) in a blood-curdling voice. Despite being hog-tied and face down on the ground, clearly posing no threat to the authorities, he is kicked and mercilessly beaten by a gang of Border Patrol agents. While my students saw this as clearly undue punishment for an illegal border crossing, some students' perceptions changed when they learned of his prior shoplifting arrest or drug use. Assertions of his "criminality" effectively distracted them from the horrendous, illegal, inhumane circumstances surrounding his death.

The criminalization of migrants allows Americans to easily dismiss the disturbing, violent, and illegal treatment of undocumented immigrants who break the law, drawing a neat line between them and "model migrants": people who go to college and grad school or complete military service. In other words, a distinction is made between immigrants. Those who don't fit some preconceived notion of an upstanding worker are rendered undeserving of legal protection or, worse, deserving of abuse.

The label of criminality works in a peculiar way, excluding those thus labeled from our collective understanding of humanity. Maybe this is why it was easy for so many Americans to dismiss the fact that, even though the city of New Orleans was evacuated before Hurricane Katrina hit in 2005, prisoners at Orleans Parish Prison were *not* evacuated.[44] Many of these inmates were locked up for inability to pay traffic tickets or marijuana-related offenses. If we think of these individuals as somehow *criminal*, deserving their fate, we no longer have to deal with the fact that they were kept without food for days, many of them endlessly treading water, several drowning.

This dismissal of an entire sector of our population—those deemed *criminal*—becomes vastly more disturbing when we think about what counts as a crime in the United States. Wearing the wrong color T-shirt, sharing food in public, falling asleep under a bridge[45]—each of these infractions could ostensibly make you a "criminal." As a criminal, you would become one of the unfortunate victims of not only the American *legal* system but also the American social imaginary. Each of these "crimes" makes your drowning in a prison cell or being fatally beaten at the US-Mexico border seem somehow more reasonable, less atrocious, and perhaps even more deserved in the eyes of the general public. After all, you're a criminal.

"I COULD GET IN SOME KIND OF TROUBLE"

Asad, one of the men I'd interviewed in depth for my field research years ago, met up with me in Philadelphia recently. He found himself perusing my books, many of them related to the war on terror, race, and Islamophobia. He came across a book, *Dirty Wars*, by investigative journalist Jeremy Scahill.[46] "What's this one about?" he asked.

I explained to him that Scahill writes a chilling account of secret US military operations around the world. Scahill explores how George W. Bush used these covert ops, funded through top-secret "black budgets," and Barack Obama expanded their use. Asad looked at the book, a hefty tome of more than five hundred pages, and told me that the topic sounded interesting, but he'd never be able to get through a book that long.

> "They made a documentary movie about it, actually, if you'd rather watch that," I told him. "It's on Netflix."
>
> "I don't want to watch that," he said. "You never know, you watch this thing. They keep records of everything. They see I watched it. I could get in some kind of trouble."

Asad was dissuaded from watching an Oscar-nominated documentary about a topic in which he takes a keen interest. This tells us about the indirect impact of the ever-lurking surveillance apparatus in the lives of many US Muslims. Asad understands that "they" keep records, and that "they" could get him in trouble just for watching a movie. Asad was right. Consider Section 215 of the Patriot Act, which allowed the FBI to secretly monitor the library books people were checking out, endangering library users' constitutional and privacy rights.[47] Sunaina Marr Maira describes Muslim youths' awareness about surveillance, saying that "the fear of surveillance becomes internalized so that it produces a regulatory apparatus through auto-censorship, without the need for state repression."[48]

American Muslims often proudly proclaim that they have "nothing to hide"; they're not afraid of surveillance. After all, they haven't done anything wrong. Yet profiling and infiltration do something beyond just sniffing out criminals: they instill deep distrust and paranoia among those they target. The experiences of civil rights activists, spied on and infiltrated far more than our schoolbooks would have us think, show us just how much infiltration breeds distrust, leads to schisms, and effectively halts political organizing. The scholar Manning Marable wrote a biography of hundreds of pages on the life of Malcolm X, drawing largely from declassified data from the extensive surveillance file that was kept on him.[49] Every detail about Malcolm X's life—including private information about his sexuality and his marriage—was intimately familiar to the FBI and NYPD. Marable's biography documents the use of African American FBI agents to document Malcolm X's every move. One informant noted that he had a

> strong hatred for the blue eyed devils, but this hatred is not likely to erupt in violence as he is much too clever and intelligent for that. He is fearless and cannot be intimidated by words or threats of personal harm. He has most of the answers at his fingertips and should be carefully dealt with. He is not likely to violate any ordinances or laws. He neither smokes nor drinks and is of high moral character.[50]

The Bureau was reading his letters, bugging his hotel rooms, and sending spies to report back on his leadership role. Unsure of who was a spy, who was an enemy, who was trustworthy, which rooms were bugged, and which phones were tapped, Malcolm was driven by government surveillance to a tortured paranoia.

Now consider the group of Muslim college students who took a whitewater-rafting trip in upstate New York in 2008. These students were later shocked to discover that one of the eighteen students was an undercover NYPD officer taking close notes on who was present, what was being discussed, the religiosity of each student, and more. Imagine the impact of such a discovery on college students, who often find the university campus to be a place to build community. Knowing that even a weekend trip is monitored, infiltrated, and policed is sure to instill deep distrust. In my research, I met many Muslim Americans who avoided such events for the very reason that they didn't want to be placed on any watchlist. One Hunter College Muslim Student Association (MSA) member told the UK *Guardian*, "I saw a sign up that said, 'Please refrain from having political conversations in MSA.'"[51] While joining student groups is generally applauded as a form of civic engagement and extracurricular involvement, for Muslims it's a reminder that they are inherently suspect. "Our MSA tries to keep it nonpolitical," Aisha, an Ohio college student and active MSA member, told me at a convention in Cincinnati. "We keep it on the level of, you know, getting together for meals and holidays and talking about cultural matters. We don't get political. That's not our goal and, you know . . . it could bring the wrong kind of attention to us." In many MSAs, this is a divisive issue. There are members who believe that the organization *ought* to be actively engaged on matters of politics and social justice, and those who think it would be safer, savvier, and more strategic to avoid that altogether. And for many Muslim students, knowing these groups are watched is enough to deter them from joining.

THE VISUAL POLITICS OF 9/11

We can learn a great deal about power, authority, and status in a society by thinking about what is viewed and what is hidden from sight. Consider the visual politics around media coverage of 9/11. By "visual politics," I mean what is watched and who does the watching. The images of the Twin Towers burning, the horrific sight of people leaping out of the top floors of the building to their death, and the stunning images of planes flying directly into the skyscrapers have become emblazoned in our collective memory. You would be hard-pressed to find someone who cannot vividly recall these images, whether or not they actually remember 9/11. Images of the attacks were heavily broadcast and circulated, played and replayed, around the world. Many young Americans' understanding of their nation has taken shape against the backdrop of 9/11, images that many had only imagined as appropriate for the Hollywood screen.[52] To my students, many of whom grew up in the "terror age," it seems appropriate that the Twin Towers' collapse should occupy so much airtime. It was a unique tragedy, they tell me. It was exceptional in its horror; it marked a new age in US politics.

Each of these claims might be true. Yet just a few years later, when a comparable number of Americans died and a vast number were permanently displaced in the devastation of Hurricane Katrina, the images of a child floating face down in floodwater and of vigilante white militias shooting black men who were seeking help did not become quintessential images of American suffering. Certainly not the way those images of 9/11 did. Or consider the government ban on the media showing images of the coffins of soldiers who lost their lives in the months following the 2003 invasion of Iraq. Some thought this ban was meant to protect viewers from traumatic and disturbing images. Yet why play and replay disturbing images of New Yorkers leaping to their deaths, only to then censor images that remind us of the soldiers who lost their lives in Iraq?

What *gets to count* as a national tragedy is the product of decisions, often made from the highest seats of power. Certain things are rendered spectacles, while others remain out of sight. The abundance of traumatic images of the United States "under attack" pushes us to see the United States as a unique type of victim.[53] As Gilbert Achcar says, the media coverage of 9/11 was "overdramatized . . . the result of deliberate action by media."

The repeated bombardment of 9/11 imagery most certainly had an impact on the collective American psyche. Seeing the nation as under attack, witnessing vivid scenes of desperation and victimhood, shaped Americans' political demands. These visual politics made possible the widespread manipulation of public opinion.[54] Seeing themselves as victimized or assaulted by barbaric terrorists, Americans were expected to imagine that they were living under a state of exception, that things were so dangerous and volatile that even our established rights could be ignored or erased altogether.

Consider the system of color-coded terror alerts that adorned airport security areas in the years following 9/11. Also known as the Homeland

Security Advisory System, these color codes were meant to indicate the current threat level—low, guarded, elevated, high, severe. Each of these "threat levels" mapped onto a different color that was boldly posted in airports for passengers to see as they passed through security on any given day. Seeing the alert level "red" (severe) would mean—what? Panicked passengers? Increased patience for longer lines at security? Heightened support for racial profiling? It's hard to say. When I teach about the color-coded alert system, my students—most of whom are too young to remember it—have a hearty laugh. They see it as a hilarious manipulation of public fear, relief, and anxiety at airports—a psychological ploy. They also say it sounds massively ineffective in fighting a terrorist threat. But in its heyday, it was no laughing matter. It was considered a serious mechanism for keeping America's travelers safe.

LIFE IN THE PANOPTICON

My students know surveillance mechanisms are widespread. They make offhand statements about the government reading our emails, about how everything one does on Facebook is monitored by the state, and about how there is no such thing as privacy anymore. That Big Brother is watching is a foregone conclusion. I teach about modern panopticism (that is, how a small, powerful elite can keep watch—often covertly—over large populations). The classroom conversation, without fail, goes like this:

> I ask, "So where are there surveillance cameras?"
> "Banks." "Subway platforms." "ATMs." "Elevators."
> And then, every time, consistently, a student will chime in: "Surveillance cameras are *everywhere*."

But *are* they everywhere? Were there cameras in the boardrooms in 2016 when execs decided to hire TigerSwan, a private security firm, to use counterterrorism tactics against Native Americans protesting the illegal Dakota Access Pipeline?[55] There certainly weren't video cameras monitoring the conversations among NYPD employees who decided to show thousands of officers a deeply racist, anti-Muslim film as part of their training.[56] (This might be why the NYPD was able to deny it had screened the film, lying about it until the *Village Voice* proved that the video *had* indeed been used.)

Students' inevitable knee-jerk response, "Surveillance cameras are *everywhere*," is only partially true. Far from being everywhere, surveillance mechanisms neatly—by design—dodge spaces where power, authority, and wealth are concentrated. This is the most important lesson of hypervisibility: that the scrutiny of being watched is, for those who are watched, suffocating. Privilege means the ability to avoid watchful eyes; oppression means being unable to escape them.

In this chapter, we have seen just how critical the realm of the visual is. Our consumption of images of terror attacks on television or of reminders at airport security (be they color-coded alerts or reminders to be aware of suspicious activity) are not politically neutral activities. To understand the politics of *watching* is to begin to make sense of how power works. For many Muslims, the realities of surveillance and policing leave an indelible mark on everyday life. We have seen how this has been the case for countless people of color. Hypervisibility is a burden of race. The ability to watch over others—as state officials, as curious neighbors, or as conscientious citizens—is itself an enactment of racism.

3

MUSLIM BEAUTY QUEENS AND THE MASTER NARRATIVE

"To quote *Scarface*," said Wajahat Ali, Muslim American comedian, spokesperson, and lawyer, "'first you get the money, then you get the power, then you get the women.'" A ripple of laughter spread through the audience at the Islam in America conference.

> Well, we didn't just get any woman. We got *the* woman. We nabbed Miss USA. We put a tiara on Rima Fakih. That was a huge success in the Muslim culture war. We have placed hummus and tahini in supermarkets, and white hipsters eat it every day. Hipsters have also made the keffiyeh[1] into a fashion statement. When hipsters fall at the feet of Muslim fashion, the world is next. We are now officially as American as apple pie and Snooki.[2]

As we saw in the previous chapter, US Muslims are hypervisible subjects, scrutinized by both ordinary people and the powers that be. But for many, life isn't just about being *under* the microscope. In fact, especially for the organizations I researched, there's an active engagement *with* the microscope. As one of my interlocutors put it, "If we're in the spotlight, that just means it's our turn to shine." In the documentary *The Muslims Are Coming!* comedian Jon Stewart says, "What a great moment for Muslims, because everyone's eyes are upon you. When eyes are upon you, that's when people see you as human."[3] Many Muslims, especially spokespeople and organizational leaders, have echoed this sentiment, suggesting that this environment of hypervisibility means Muslims can take advantage of the spotlight to present a favorable image of Islam. California-based Muslim American scholar Zaid Shakir said to a room full of hundreds of attendees that Muslims must build a positive image. "Let us leave the Gingriches of the world. Let God deal with them. If we do that, there will be less who serve as an audience for bigotry. Instead, they'll say, 'Hey, those people gave me free medical treatment.'" He puts on a fake "white-rural" accent. "'I love me some Moslems,' they'll say." Many Muslim American advocacy groups have been engaged in a process of showing America that Muslims are *not* terrorists, *not* foreign entities—in short, that they are not the Other.

UNDERSTANDING ETHNONATIONALISM

When Rima Fakih was crowned 2010's Miss USA, she said, "I'd like to say that I'm American first, and I am Arab American, I am Lebanese American, and I am Muslim American."[4] Fakih's win had far-reaching implications, with some arguing that her "integration by bikini could go a long way toward demonstrating to Americans that Muslims are not a weirdly frightening, monolithic group, and thus begin to break down prejudice."[5] (Fakih has since converted to Christianity.) But not all reactions to Fakih's win were so positive; some saw her victory as part of a climate of "pandering" to Muslims, while others spoke conspiratorially of her ties to Hezbollah. Regardless, people from across the political spectrum were reading into the significance of her victory. Writer Ahmed Rehab wrote, "That her religion is even brought up is only indicative of how far our unhealthy obsession with this age-old faith and its adherents has gone."[6] Rehab points to the fact that Fakih's win—lauded by integrationists, shunned by antipageant feminists, deemed shameful by religious conservatives—couldn't exist as simply another beauty-pageant victory. It was pregnant with meaning for the significance of Islam in America. "She won a beauty contest, and now she's being looked upon as an ambassador of her religion," said Detroit-based imam Dawud Walid.[7] And when Ibtihaj Muhammad, the first Olympic athlete to wear a hijab, competed in fencing in the Summer 2016 games, a similar public conversation about Muslim women and Islam in America surfaced.

Yet one doesn't have to be a crowned beauty queen or an Olympic athlete to be asked to be an informal ambassador of Islam. On the contrary; even *ordinary* Muslims find themselves speaking for Muslims at large. As such, they are caught in a tricky act of leveraging their hypervisibility, negotiating the spotlight they find themselves thrust into to prove their Americanness, their peacefulness, or their modernity. "I can't run a stop sign and not have it reflect badly on Muslims," Amina told me at a conference in Chicago. "I wear a hijab. It's not just that I'm afraid of the consequences for *myself* when I mess up—say, if I scold my son for throwing a tantrum in a mall, or if I accidentally cut someone off in traffic. It's like you're always on your best behavior because, if you're not, it's going to end up screwing a lot of people." Another young woman reported,

> Every Muslim has to do their own PR campaign. It's really weird. I don't know if this happens to you. But if I'm in a place where I have a choice to open a door for somebody or not, I'll err toward opening the door. Not because I feel courteous but because I'm like, this white person is watching me. And if I open the door for them, it's like one more point for Muslims. It's weird to have to think that way. And in the back of my head, there's this mental process. Little things, hold the elevator door or don't hold it. Maybe if it's a brown, Muslim person, I'd be like whatever. But if it's a white person . . . you may be *the* Muslim person they see. Little things like that.

Leveraging hypervisibility has meant, for many, being on the defensive, always ready to respond to an overarching climate of anti-Muslim hostility. Among those I studied, collectively shouldering a burden for an entire population has often meant showing America that Islam does, indeed, belong here. The organizations I study have been busy excavating a history that is often forgotten: the history of Muslim contributions to the United States. Countless "Islam in America"–themed events, for instance, inevitably reference the "ice cream cone" story. Linah explained it to me as we stood in the bazaar section of an Islamic convention, though I'd heard it before. "In 1904, a Muslim Arab man was selling Syrian waffles at the World's Fair in St. Louis. Next to him, an Italian was selling gelato. The Italian dude ran out of cups. So the Arab guy rolled up one of his waffles, suggested he use that to serve his ice cream, and voilà! The ice cream cone was invented!" The tale of the ice cream cone resurfaced in speeches, panels, publications, and my own personal conversations with attendees at such events. The telling and retelling of this story is meant to prove that Muslims *do* in fact belong—for what could be more American than an ice cream cone?

Such reminders that Muslims have deep roots in America are offered as a challenge. They are meant to contest the *master narrative* of American history.[8] The master narrative is the general belief that the United States is a nation founded by and belonging to white, English-speaking, Euro-American Christians. This is why calls to "go back to your country" are hurled at Asian Americans bicycling through their neighborhoods in California,[9] but *not* at Polish Americans. Though many of California's Asians have been there since the 1800s, they are perceived as more "immigrant-like" than more recent white arrivals. They are, as Timothy Fong says, perpetual foreigners.[10] Through the master narrative, a mythology takes shape, a mythology of what is and isn't "American." It is this narrative that determines which stories land at the center of a page, which are pushed to its margins, and which are ignored altogether.

The master narrative renders invisible countless enslaved Africans, and the Muslim roots many of them brought to the Americas; it erases the fact that Muslim navigators were on board Columbus's ships. The master narrative allows us to overlook those in formerly Mexican territories in the American Southwest who say, "We didn't cross the border, the border crossed us." The master narrative may explain why several of these *American citizens* were deported en masse in the 1930s, during the era of Mexican repatriation—a law based on *race*, not citizenship. (It wouldn't be until the year 2005 that California formally apologized to Mexicans for repatriation.) The master narrative, in other words, does a lot of erasing and rewriting of history in order to offer up the "fact" of a white Christian America.

Yet the master narrative is firmly entrenched. It exists not only in the minds of those who wish to restore America to some imagined Euro-American past but also in the textbooks that teach us American history. This is why college students come into my class knowing full well about the Irish potato famine and the huge waves of Irish migration to the United States but so few know about Japanese settlement in the Hawaiian islands for work on sugar plantations. Fewer still know of the influx of Arabs in the early 1900s to towns like Paterson, New Jersey, where they established a robust textile industry.

To understand the master narrative is to begin to understand ethno-nationalism. Ethnonationalism is the view that a nation ought to be comprised of a particular ethnic, religious, and/or linguistic community. Those who are not of that heritage are expected to either assimilate or be excluded. That ethnonationalism is an integral part of American race politics should come as no surprise to any student of history. While many know 1492 as the year Columbus "sailed the ocean blue," it was also the year of the Spanish expulsion. The very King Ferdinand and Queen Isabella who financed Columbus's voyage also deemed that Spain, which had been ruled for centuries by Moorish Muslims, must purge Muslims and Jews from its newly formed Catholic state. Ramon Grosfoguel reminds us that "1492 is a crucial foundational year for the understanding of our *present* system."[11] He explains how this ethnona-tionalist moment in Spain came to be, in a sense, the backbone of how European modernity would understand *nations* as belonging to particu-lar *groups*: ethnic, religious, or (eventually) racial. It is telling that the very discovery of the New World (by Europe, that is) happened at the same moment as the creation of this ethnically "pure" new Spanish state. Ethnonationalism, then, was alive and well in the European worldview at the time the Americas were colonized.

In order to maintain a belief in ethnonationalism, what must be ignored (whether it's fifteenth-century Spain or the present-day United States) is a basic fact of human history: that humans have moved. The human story is a long tale of cross-cultural contact, migration, and transcultural learning. Groups of people from all corners of the world have influenced one another's ways of living so extensively that it's impossible to draw boundaries around what a culture, nation, or relig-ion *is*. Perhaps this is why the ice cream cone story keeps coming up: Is the ice cream cone American? Is it Arab? Is it *Muslim*? Does it matter? Cultural contact, migration, and sharing are all part and parcel of the process of cultural diffusion, through which cultures come to be. In order to create a master narrative, such histories must be wiped out and erased, and new ones rewritten and propagated.

Yet ethnonationalist movements are intensifying globally, not just in the United States. It might be helpful here to consider what's happened in India with the rise of Hindu ethnonationalism. India, which suffered brutal British colonialism, includes diverse communities that settled over the centuries. They came from Persia, southeast Africa, Afghanistan, China, and beyond. India is populated by Hindus, Muslims (both Shi'a and Sunni), Christians (Protestant, Catholic, and Orthodox), Sikhs, and Buddhists, among many others. Each of these populations contributed to India's architecture, cuisine, landscape, and linguistitics. In order to effectively rule over this vast territory, the British often fanned the flames of sectarianism and religious hatred, pitting Hindu against Muslim. (Such divide-and-conquer tactics have been requisites for colonial rule everywhere.) So, when the British were expelled in 1947, they left in their wake deep rivalries between Hindus and Muslims. These rivalries, which led to an ultimate rift between India and Pakistan, continue to this day. Far from being primordial or hardwired into India's two main religious groups, these divisions are *political*. In other words, there's nothing *inherent* or *natural* about the Hindu-Muslim rivalries we see today. Yet ethnonationalist Hindus tell an origin story of India as an essentially Hindu nation—an origin story referred to as *Hindutva*. In doing so, they wipe clean the memory of its rich religious and ethnic diversity. This process has reached fever pitch in recent decades, with ethnonationalism guiding widespread anti-Muslim pogroms in India. Airports with Muslim names have been renamed with quintessentially Hindu ones. In 2017, Hindu nationalists tried to claim that the Taj Mahal was built not by the Muslim emperor Shah Jahan but by Hindus—a claim so ludicrous that it was easily disproven by archaeologists.[12] Indian history textbooks have been revised to minimize or delete Muslims' presence. As a result, when today's young Indians grow up having been taught this version of history, calls to "purify" India to its pristine Hindu past will seem perfectly sensible. After all, India's master narrative has become one of Hindutva.

I offer the example of India to shed light on the ethnonationalist movement in the United States. In 2016, hordes of American voters were compelled to "make America great again" (MAGA) in 2016. The campaign slogan of Donald Trump's presidential campaign, MAGA relies on a fundamentally ethnonationalist logic. Supporters of MAGA wish to return to the good old days when, as Trump pointed out when a protestor appeared at his rally, "they'd be carried out on a stretcher, folks."[13] Perhaps the greatest dog whistle of our time, the MAGA movement has upset liberals, who ask *which* America it is that Trump would like to see restored. Is it the one of legalized segregation, as in Jim Crow laws in the South? Is it the long legacy of racial terror, where the government overlooked entire white communities coming together to lynch Mexicans for celebrating their holidays or black men for wearing their military uniforms?[14] Is it racist immigration legislation, such as the racist Chinese Exclusion Act?

But to blame MAGA, the Trump campaign, or the Republican Party for ethnonationalism is to miss the mark entirely, to overlook the fact that ethnonationalism is *America's* common sense. Indeed, the very textbooks our young people read about US history and politics reinforce the master narrative. It wasn't the Trump campaign that deleted from our national memory the state-sanctioned murder of Fred Hampton. It wasn't the Republican Party that kept out of popular education the racial solidarity exercised by John Brown. (If you don't know either of those names, my point is proven.) To regard MAGA's ethnonationalism as exceptional when it is, in fact, commonplace, is to leave us armed with nothing but with weak-kneed defenses invoking Muslim beauty queens and the mainstreaming of keffiyehs.

CONTESTING THE MASTER NARRATIVE

Those whom the master narrative erases or marginalizes often expend great energy trying to revise, topple, or falsify it. Consider the book by Imam Feisal Abdul Rauf, who spearheaded the "Ground Zero mosque" project. *What's Right with Islam Is What's Right with America* argues that liberty, equality, and social justice are constitutional values just as much as they are Islamic ones. What Abdul Rauf's book offers is something called a *counternarrative*, a distinct response to the master narrative's exclusion of Muslims and other people of color.

Hamza Yusuf, a Muslim American scholar and celebrity spokesperson, spoke in Washington, DC, in 2012. "When we think of the US," he said, "we have to know that *we* are a part of this story. Muslims are a part of this narrative, and have been a part of this narrative from the beginning. America is a story of immigrants, and you are part of that story. Those of you who came later, you must see yourselves as part of that story." Yusuf, a white convert to Islam, was asking Muslims—African American, Arab, South and Southeast Asian—to *Americanize*

Islam, to see it as anything *but* foreign. He too offered a counternarrative. Yusuf reminded his audience that Thomas Jefferson himself owned a Quran and hosted an *iftar* at his residence in 1805, and that world-famous athlete Muhammad Ali was Muslim. In another speech, Yusuf told hundreds of attendees, "Muslims fought in all of these wars in American history. We fought for this country in World War II, in World War I, in the Civil War. So this idea that we're alien is completely unacceptable."

Newsweek describes Yusuf as follows:

> Born Mark Hanson, the son of California intellectuals, Yusuf was baptized in the Greek Orthodox Church and raised on a '70s diet of surfing and spiritual eclecticism. At 18, having narrowly survived a car crash, he started reading intently about Islamic spirituality. Over the next 10 years, he studied classical Islamic law and theology in Algeria, Mauritania and Morocco. Today he is as comfortable speaking Arabic on Al-Jazeera as he is expounding on American TV. His dazzling dexterity with Qur'anic knowledge and thinkers from Aristophanes to Mark Twain has made him a great popularizer of the faith.[15]

The article goes on to highlight Yusuf's appeal to Muslims and non-Muslims alike; he serves as a bridge between both groups. He "wants Westerners to reform their relationship with the Islamic world, and Muslims to reform their own society . . . When an ex-surfer from the Bay Area can become a Muslim authority, it's a sign that the West is now part of the Muslim world, too." Yusuf stands as an embodiment of the fact that Islam *is* American. But there are controversies surrounding Yusuf: many felt he had "sold out" after 9/11 for visiting the White House to speak with Bush in an amicable meeting, earning him the nickname "Hamza Useless." In 2016, controversy around Yusuf erupted again when he minimized the role of anti-black racism in American policing, referencing statistics about black-on-black crime and reciting claims about how police murders of black people cannot be uniformly regarded as racist. But Yusuf remains a unique figure in Muslim American representation—a white convert to Islam who enjoys celebrity status among members of these groups. Yusuf, alongside a whole host of other white Muslim converts who became prominent Muslim community leaders, stands as a reminder to the American mainstream that Islam need not be brown, black, foreign, or migrant. Whitening Islam means making it palatable for America.

In fact, Americanizing Islam is a major preoccupation of many anti-Islamophobia advocates. In a conversation with Sumaiya, a New Yorker I met while doing my fieldwork, she reminded me of just how many English words come from Arabic. "Think about it: *algebra, alcohol, cotton.*" Sumaiya thus demonstrated the undeniable interconnections between the West and the Muslim world. Countless Muslim organizations have printed and circulated pamphlets enumerating the contributions Muslims have made to the West, to the United States, to science, or to art.

Even non-Muslims participate in issuing these countless reminders that Muslims have shaped the modern world and American culture in undeniable ways. President Obama, in a speech to the "Muslim world" in Cairo, said,

> America and Islam are not exclusive, and need not be in competition. Instead, they overlap, and share common principles—principles of justice and progress; tolerance and the dignity of all human beings. . . . And since our founding, American Muslims have enriched the United States. They have fought in our wars, served in government, stood for civil rights, started businesses, taught at our Universities, excelled in our sports arenas, won Nobel Prizes, built our tallest building, and lit the Olympic Torch.[16]

This Muslim counternarrative of inclusion can only be understood as a *response.* I doubt Muslims would so repeatedly, laboriously remind the public of their contributions to America were it not for their experience of deep hostility and systemic exclusion. What the Islamophobia industry[17] does is cast Muslims as outsiders, foreigners, incompatible with everything Western, everything modern. Organizations like Stop Islamization of America have placed billboard-sized anti-Muslim ads on the sides of city buses. Islamophobia has thus become a literal, visible feature of urban space. Talk-show host Bill Maher said of practicing Muslims, "They're violent. They threaten us. They bring that *desert stuff* to our world. *We* don't threaten each other. We sue each other. That's the sign of civilized people."[18] Even a liberal talk-show host, then, is easily able to draw a line between us and them, modern and savage, civilized and barbaric. Such anti-Muslim venom is at once the backdrop to and the inspiration for these Muslim counternarratives.

When I see community groups expending vast amounts of energy to offer and propagate Muslim counternarratives, I bristle. Not because those narratives are false; far from it. As an anthropologist, tracing the diverse and often surprising histories of our art, science, poetry, and architecture is always striking. These histories reveal remarkable moments in the human story. Jerk chicken, now served up in American food courts, was invented by those who fled slavery in Jamaica, hid in the mountains, and had to find ways to prepare their food in secrecy so as not to be detected by slave masters. Shampoo, an Indian invention, is now a part of everyday hygiene in the West. It's not just the ice cream cone; the most prosaic items in our everyday lives tell tales that reveal complex histories of human contact. They stand as proof that the world's cultures are not pure but hybrid, the product of far-flung people's encounters and collisions.

So I am not critical of the Muslim counternarrative; I am critical of the defensiveness that inspires it. It seems that, in mainstream discourse, we only have one of two choices in talking about Islam or Muslims: make an anti-Muslim or bigoted statement, pointing to the barbaric savagery of Islam, *or* make a claim about what Edward Said calls "Islam's humanism, its contribution to civilization, development, and moral righteousness."[19] Islamophobes insult Islam; those who object to Islamophobia sing its praises. Islamophobes claim that Muslim women are oppressed; defenders of Muslims respond with trite examples of the rights guaranteed to women under Islam. This debate omits the fact of a global patriarchy that permeates all major religious traditions. (The West regards as *especially* barbaric the rare practice of "honor killings" in certain Muslim societies, less obsessed with the fact of overwhelming intimate partner violence and murder in our own part of the world.) A volley between those slandering Islam and those singing its praises is not a terribly fruitful debate. It is, instead, a conversation confined by the poles of offensiveness and defensiveness.

Maybe this defensiveness is why typing "Muslim contributions" into Google yields the autocomplete options "to the world," "to medicine," "to science," and "to America." Maybe this is why a *1001 Inventions* exhibit reminds attendees that Muslims invented modern surgery, coffee, and even the mathematics required for modern computers and smartphones.[20] In my fieldwork, I heard constant refrains of the myriad contributions Muslims have made to American life: the Willis Tower skyscraper in Chicago, for instance, which long stood as the world's tallest building, designed by Muslim architect Fazlur Rahman Khan.[21] When Americans gathered to watch the solar eclipse in the summer of 2017, many Muslims were quick to remind the public that the pinhole camera box many people use to watch solar eclipses was invented by a Muslim man in the tenth century. Many think these reminders, proof that Muslims have undoubtedly contributed to the rich tapestry of American culture, the presence of Muslim beauty queens and athletes, will defeat Islamophobia.

Will they?

4

NEOLIBERALISM AND THE GOOD
MUSLIM ARCHETYPE

For Muslims who find themselves backed into a corner, forced to prove to the mainstream that they are worthy of *being*, offering constant reminders to the public that they are architects and doctors, that they have helped shape US cuisine and literature and medicine, Islamophobia has been a hefty distraction. The Islamophobia industry has set the very terms of the debate around Islam and Muslims. Against accusations that they are barbaric, backward, or innately violent, it seems that all Muslims can do is try to prove they are not. Muslims would not be so eager to produce this trove of evidence of Islam's positive history and potential were it not being so viciously tarnished. This is why the "good Muslim" strategy, or Islamophilia, is particularly troubling. The counternarratives discussed in chapter 3 are but one example of Islamophilia, which can take many forms. As we will see, the arguments that Muslims are active contributors to civilization, that they are patriotic Americans, or that they stand staunchly against acts of terrorism constitute unique, sometimes overlapping, forms of Islamophilia.

ISLAMOPHILIA

My research reveals that many Muslim spokespeople and national-level organizations have opted for an Islamophilic route to combat Islamophobia. Zareena Grewal argues that "Muslim American leaders-turned-spokespeople affirm their positive identification with the US as good, flag-waving citizens, identifying Islam in terms of normative definitions of a good religion and claiming a space in the cultural mainstream through the disavowal and identification of bad Muslims and bad Islam."[1] Islamophilia thus attempts to take what is painted as a treacherous, hostile, or foreign Islam and repackage it in ways acceptable to the West.[2]

I had just given a talk at a public library in New Jersey. An elderly white woman sitting in the front row raised her hand during the question-and-answer session following my lecture. "I've really enjoyed your talk," she started.

> But let me just share this experience I had at the farmer's market. I was there a few months ago, and I was, perhaps somewhat rudely, inadvertently staring at a young Muslim woman in a headscarf. She caught me staring, so I smiled. I was embarrassed. She smiled back, and we went our separate ways, shopping. When I got to the cash register, the cashier told me that my groceries had been paid for. The Muslim woman had paid for my groceries! I caught up with her in the parking lot and told her that wasn't necessary. She was just so sweet. I insisted on taking her to lunch. We had a lovely lunch together. I think it was my first time sitting to eat with a Muslim person. It never would have happened if she hadn't taken that step, the step of being kind in the face of my rudeness.

I was stunned and, frankly, a bit upset. Are Muslims expected to buy gallons of milk for people who ogle them in public spaces? Is that the price to pay to be seen as human? Is *that* how anti-Muslim hysteria will be defeated?

My irritation at the question speaks to a much larger concern. I worry that, in all our talk about the virulent presence of *anti*-Muslim bigotry, we forget the troubling role of trying to prove yourself legitimate in a nation that has cast you as Other. In this chapter, we can begin to think about *responses* to Islamophobia, specifically responses that attempt to prove that not all Muslims are terrorists, that *some* Muslims ought to be included in the United States, or that many Muslims are exceptional or upstanding citizens. This is the type of response that argues that Islam is essentially a peaceful religion or that Muslims do immeasurable good for America as hardworking and upstanding citizens.

That Muslims are hardworking, peace-loving Americans is an oft-repeated claim by those who would like to see Islamophobia defeated. Shining a spotlight on Muslims who condemn terror and pledge deep allegiance to the US flag, they think, will challenge Islamophobia. A few days after 9/11, President Bush said, "America counts millions of Muslims among our citizens, and Muslims make an incredibly valuable contribution to our country. Muslims are doctors, lawyers, shopkeepers, moms and dads, and they need to be treated with respect."[3] He added, "Muslims love America as much as I do."

When Obama delivered his speech to the "Muslim world" in Cairo, he too lauded the positive values and contributions of Muslims (certain Muslims). Which Muslims, I wonder, were the intended audience? Was it residents of Mogadishu, the Somali city ravaged by warfare and famine, much of it wrought by the United States? Was it business students at elite American universities, many of them members of the organizations I studied in my fieldwork? Was it the robust black Muslim population in North Philadelphia, where some of America's most historic mosques are located? Even terms like *Muslim-majority countries* or *the MENA region* (Middle East/North Africa) don't *usefully* describe a "Muslim world." It's hard to find appropriate language to describe a billion and a half human beings. There's no coherence to these labels; each of them falls critically short. A vast global population of Muslims gets flattened under this label, preventing us from seeing its rifts and schisms.

When Trump's "Muslim ban" first went into effect, Nisrin Elamin spoke to the media about her experience attempting to travel back to the United States during the ban. Elamin, a Sudanese PhD student in anthropology at Stanford University, put it plainly: "I was probably treated much better than other people, partly because of my affiliation with Stanford. I think that led to me being detained for five hours, as opposed to another Sudanese person who was detained for thirty hours, and he is in his seventies."[4] Elamin's comments remind us that Islamophobia's effects aren't felt evenly across Muslim populations. Class and cultural capital play a key role in sheltering some Muslims from the full effect of Islamophobia and exposing others to the brunt of it. The way the Muslim ban was discussed by the general public revealed this divide between Muslims *deserving* of sympathy and welcome in the United States and the undeserving—those worthy of exclusion and suspicion. Tech professionals in Silicon Valley, for instance, spoke out against the Muslim ban. They reminded the public that it would block talented workers from entering the United States. The media provided profiles of such Muslims impacted by the travel ban, including researchers at Google, product designers at Facebook, or employees at Pinterest.[5] Arizona senator John McCain spoke out against the travel ban, upset that those who had been key in the US war effort in Iraq would be impacted. (Eventually, Iraq would be removed from the list of "banned" countries.) In opposition to the Muslim ban, everywhere there were reminders of Muslims' instrumental role in the US economy and military. *That*, it was argued, was why the ban ought to be opposed.

Resistance to the travel ban picked up such widespread momentum in part because its "victims" were seen as PhD students and software developers: people the US economy cannot stand to lose. This might explain the disparity between the huge protests against Trump's travel ban and the relative silence around the National Security Entry-Exit Registration System (NSEERS) that had been in place under Bush and Obama. NSEERS, implemented as a terrorism prevention tool in the wake of 9/11, also singled out Muslims for a fingerprinting and registry system. The ACLU deemed it racist and discriminatory. Yet there was very little in the way of widespread public outcry, nothing like the veritable uprising that took place against the travel ban.

The "deserving versus undeserving" divide is useful for making sense of the good Muslim/bad Muslim framework. Consider how many think about America's poor. In popular discourse, poor people are thought to be poor for one of two reasons: either because of circumstances beyond their control, or due directly to their own flawed life choices. The first—the deserving poor—might be eligible for subsidized housing or food stamps. After all, their poverty is no fault of their own. The others, though, are seen as singularly responsible for their own plight due to their sexual practices, their family structure, their relationship to drugs, or their criminal past and thus unworthy of any social welfare or even public sympathy. For instance, legislation forcing food-stamp recipients to pass a drug test separates out those who "deserve" these benefits from those who don't. Such requirements ignore the troubling relationship between poverty, addiction, and mass incarceration.

While much ink has been spilled about the "deserving and undeserving" poor, less has been written about the deserving or undeserving *Muslim*. When efforts to fight Islamophobia focus on the experiences of the most elite Muslims, this division is kept intact. As we will see, it's dangerous to amplify the voices of those Muslims least impacted by anti-Muslim racism. Such efforts leave its most vulnerable victims unrepresented, unprotected, and invisible. We have seen that Muslim Americans are not a monolith. They are fractured along lines of race, class, and immigration status. We should be mindful of this as we assess the statements against Islamophobia. We must think about which Muslims are murdered, detained, and deported. And we must also think about which Muslims are given government grants, write op-eds in the mainstream media, or play quirky characters in television comedies. We must further ask what it means that such "spokespeople" are often sheltered from Islamophobia in its most egregious forms.

THE GOOD MUSLIM

The question then is, who *are* the good Muslims? What do they do that separates them out from the Muslims who are deemed a threat to the West? Are they patriotic? Are they highly educated? Do they not make outward shows of their religious practice? Do they speak vocally about their hatred for terrorism committed by Muslims? And what are the troubling side effects, perhaps unintentional, of marking *these* Muslims as "safe" or appropriate Americans?

In 2007, *Newsweek* published a cover story titled "American Dreamers" that provided a snapshot of the lives of Muslims in the United States. These success stories included Ferdous Sajedeen, owner of a lucrative pharmacy business, and cardiologist Maher Hathout. The story seemed at first blush like a refreshing take: finally, some positive media coverage of Muslims. A *BusinessWeek* piece titled "They're Muslims and Yankees, Too" highlighted several upwardly mobile, successful American Muslims. The "Yankees" featured in the article are influential lawyers, bankers, and publishing executives—success stories who embody the American dream.

One summer, after I taught a workshop about Islamophobia in New Jersey, a schoolteacher who had attended approached me. "I think Is-

lamophobia is just ludicrous," she told me. "Some of my best students
are Muslim. They are hardworking; they don't get themselves into any
trouble. Most of them go on to be pre-med students or engineers." For
her, her perception of Muslim students as gifted was the reason they
were not deserving of Islamophobia.

I once heard a speaker at an Islamic convention in Washington, DC,
address a room of several hundred attendees. He said, "Of all global
Muslims, we are in the best position to speak out. In terms of wealth, in
terms of freedom. Especially political freedom. Let us not forget that
Allah has bestowed us with a great *ni'mah* [blessing]. It would be a pity
to squander this blessing and not speak up." He urged American Muslims to leverage their economic privilege to make a change in the world.
This reflects what Zareena Grewal calls *Muslim American exceptional-
ism*, the belief that Muslim Americans are in some way special, superi-
or, or remarkable compared to global Muslim communities.[6]

Each of these instances points to what I call *markers of legitimacy*.
For the New Jersey schoolteacher, Muslim American students are especially diligent and conscientious in school. The speaker above sees Muslims as occupying a unique role with which to do good in the world.
Such markers of legitimacy are used in defense of Muslims, to make
certain Muslims acceptable and palatable to the United States. Markers
of legitimacy render certain Muslims "good," forgiven for the transgressions of terrorists.

Another marker of Muslim legitimacy is their supposed value as
consumers. Making products "Muslim-friendly" has been hailed as a
new horizon for successful business practices. The *Economist*, for instance, wrote that the education and income level of American Muslims
makes them a worthwhile market for businesses to consider. With a
London McDonald's offering halal Chicken McNuggets and Nestle offering halal-compliant products, companies can make billions by including Muslim consumers. In 2017, *Forbes* reported that financial institutions such as UBS, Deutsche Bank, and Morgan Stanley were offering
"Sharia-compliant" financial products.

A 2007 report from the Pew Research Center titled *Muslim
Americans: Middle Class and Mostly Mainstream* opened with the
statement, "A comprehensive nationwide survey of Muslim Americans
finds them to be largely assimilated, happy with their lives, and moderate with respect to many of the issues that have divided Muslims and

Westerners around the world. . . . Overwhelmingly, they believe hard work pays off in this society. This belief is reflected in Muslim American income and education levels, which generally mirror those of the general public." This may explain why, since 2016, the animus against Muslim refugees has taken on such intensity: the preexisting script celebrated the inclusion of an upwardly mobile, professional class of Muslim. The poor migrant and the refugee do not fit the success story that has been used as a marker of legitimacy for Muslim Americans.

But the reality is that US Muslims don't belong to one racial group or one socioeconomic class. They are stratified into rigid class and race hierarchies, like the rest of the country. In his book, *American Islamophobia: Understanding the Roots and Rise of Fear*, Khaled Beydoun closely documents the disconcerting rates of poverty among Muslim populations.[7] To celebrate the wealthy American dreamers is to implicitly—sometimes explicitly—demonize those without that class status. Says Hisham Aidi, "Terrorism experts and columnists have been warning of the 'Islamic threat' in the American underclass, and alerting the public that the ghetto and the prison system could very well supply a fifth column to Osama bin Laden and his ilk."[8] In 2011, a government program called Countering Violent Extremism (CVE) created an initiative to fund health and social services to American Muslim communities, based on the idea that poverty can lead to terrorism.[9] In other words, there is a nascent fear of a Muslim threat coming out of American ghettoes: a fear of Latinx and black Muslims, refugees, and the popularity of Islam among incarcerated people. This "urban" or "ghetto" Islam has given rise to a general paranoia about an Islam that could destabilize America from below. We should think hard about the fact that this coexists with a peculiar celebration of the middle-class, professional Muslim. This demonstrates what Manning Marable calls "the problem with symbolic representation."[10] When a select few are chosen to be "representatives" of a group that is divided along class lines, their voices will often drown out the marginalized segment of that community.

NEOLIBERALISM

Neoliberalism is the philosophy that values—sanctifies, even—the privatization, the marketization, of everyday life. Neoliberalism tells us our schools and hospitals will function better if we treat them as businesses, as profit generators. It tells us that the best politicians are wealthy and have experience as businesspeople. It tells us that governments should not meddle in the workings of the "market." In short, neoliberalism tells us that accumulating wealth is a positive social value that needs no regulation or interference from the state. In fact, under neoliberalism, the government's function is to enhance the unchecked accumulation of wealth. Under neoliberalism, free markets and free competition are heralded as positive forces, likely to improve the world. Under neoliberalism, people are taught that things are best when they are allowed to behave according to the "rules of the market"—and generate the most profit along the way. This has dire consequences for social justice. Take, for instance, the bloody assault that law enforcement unleashed in 2016 against Native American protestors opposing the Dakota Access Pipeline. Under neoliberalism, the value of honoring treaties or ensuring our water is drinkable pales in comparison to the promise of the profit that an oil pipeline stands to generate.

What strikes me about neoliberalism is that it has come to be seen as obvious, natural, *the only way*. In other words, people believe that it's inevitable that the world will run according to the dictates of the profit motive. Neoliberalism has become like a second skin, influencing us on an imperceptible level.

The US racial landscape has been ingrained with neoliberal logic. I found in my research that many thought it was obvious that America would only value its Muslims if they were seen as earners and consumers. Countless interlocutors in my fieldwork made statements like "Muslims *have* to have wealth, spending power and status. *This* is how we fight Islamophobia." Some felt that this would be the *only* way to render Muslims appropriate for inclusion. As we will see, this form of *neoliberal* multiculturalism argues that diversity is "good for the bottom line."[11] Neoliberal multiculturalism is less concerned with power dynamics, history, or social justice. It is unconcerned with eradicating the very roots of inequality. Instead, issues of diversity and difference become matters of wealth and profit.

Consider what happened in 2013 when the apparel company Gap featured a turbaned Sikh actor in one of its major ads, part in a series of multiracial billboard advertisements. The ad was defaced with racial slurs such as "terrorist" and "taxi driver." In response to the vandalism, Gap released a statement claiming that "Gap is a brand that celebrates inclusion and diversity," then featured the ad as its Twitter banner image. Many applauded this move with #ThankYouGap tweets, less concerned with the company's unethical labor practices in Bangladesh (a predominantly Muslim country). Even after the deaths of hundreds of its workers in Bangladesh, Gap refused to sign on to a safety agreement. "By drawing our attention toward a single advertisement," writes Waleed Shahid, "Gap has brownwashed their own labor practices, obscuring the brown people and places from where their clothing originates." Shahid's critique is important for debunking neoliberal multiculturalism, a type of multiculturalism that is satisfied by the mere presence of nonwhite faces in advertisements, film, or boardrooms.[12]

The problem with neoliberal multiculturalism is that it keeps the underlying systems of inequality intact while maintaining a veneer of "diversity." Consider the numerous black politicians who took office in the years following the civil rights era in America. In *From #BlackLives-Matter to Black Liberation*, Keeanga-Yamahtta Taylor traces the role of black politicians in places like Ohio and Pennsylvania.[13] She juxtaposes the endurance of anti-black racism with the presence of black elected officials. Black mayors, like Carl Stokes in Cleveland or Michael Nutter in Philadelphia, maintained business-friendly policies that were bad for black communities. Yet the fact that they were black often served as a mask for their anti-black policies. And the large numbers of black cops and politicians in Baltimore did not guarantee justice in the racist murder of Freddie Gray, in which the cops were not held criminally responsible for breaking his neck.

The very presence of these "black faces in high places" allows anti-black policies to continue unchecked. As Taylor writes of the black political elite, "Their complete complicity with and absorption into the worst most corrupt aspects of American politics, including accepting donations from the most notorious corporations in the country, is not just a simple case of selling out for the sake of money and access. . . . This complicity is the price of admission into the ranks of the political establishment."[14] Yet in the aftermath of the civil rights era, many became concerned with getting black politicians elected, opting for the simple act of representation rather than any tangible shift in material practices.

MODEL MINORITIES

Similarly, Islamophilia often functions as a way to insert Muslims into the conversation simply and uncritically, without challenging the underlying realities of anti-Muslim racism. Speaking with the fashion-forward Nasreen at an Islamic convention, I remarked on her Burberry hijab. "I love me a good designer hijab, you know, with the Fendi or Chanel logo. It tells people I'm Muslim, sure, but at the same time . . . Muslims aren't backward or sloppy or anything." These conventions were indeed spectacular in their array of designer hijabs and handbags on display. The contours of class, respectability, and consumer power were made explicit in Nasreen's statement. Her designer look, she felt, was a marker of legitimacy. On another occasion, I was heading to lunch with Sarah, a young Muslim lawyer. As we walked through the parking lot, she said, "See the Mercedes and BMWs? If anyone wants to ask what we've contributed here, they just need to see the Islamic Society of North America and Islamic Circle of North America bumper stickers on these cars. This is what American Islam looks like."

As an ethnographer, I was always direct with my interlocutors about my critiques of neoliberal multiculturalism. In my effort to be up front about my differences of opinion with my fieldwork contacts, I pressed them. I asked what it meant to claim that designer hijabs or luxury sedans would shift perceptions of Muslims in America. Nasreen replied, "This is just natural. This is the story of *all* minorities in America, isn't it? They've all had to prove themselves at the American success study in order to be included. The Irish, the Jewish. They went from being discriminated against to being seen as truly American, and a large part of that was climbing the ladder. That's just how it works here." Sarah said something very similar: "I know there are lots of Muslims who can't afford these cars. But *we* can, and we get to rep the entire Muslim community." Such responses demonstrate the "taken for granted" nature of neoliberalism. Sarah and Nasreen see it as fairly obvious that consumer power and class status would *of course* be the way Muslims could "make it" in the United States.

(Yet many of the most notorious Muslim terrorists have had engineering degrees from Western universities or urban wealthy or middle-class backgrounds—not the parochial tribalists many assume them to be.[15] Al-Qaeda leader Ayman al-Zawahiri was a skilled surgeon. Osama bin Laden, hailed as the mastermind of 9/11, was from a wealthy Saudi family with strong historical ties to the US government. Anwar al-Awlaki, a preacher whose turn toward anti-Americanism got him killed in a US drone strike, was a Fulbright scholar, educated in Colorado and San Diego. It is peculiar, then, that one would use class as a marker of legitimacy.)

Muslims certainly aren't the first group to be hailed as "model" citizens or embodiments of the American dream. Let's think about Asian Americans, a group often labeled a "model minority," thought to have achieved remarkable success in the United States. Even presidents have heaped praise on Asian Americans for their positive values, hard work, and above-average median incomes.[16] That Asians are "good at math and science" or "skilled physicians" is part and parcel of the American racial vocabulary. Tune in to a TV show with a hospital scene and an Asian doctor will inevitably be featured, in spite of the relative absence of Asian actors from other television roles. The model-minority trope tells us that Asians are highly educated, technically skilled, and unaffected by the ghettoization and criminalization associated with other communities of color. At first blush, this might seem like a flattering claim. What could be wrong with being a member of a group that's "made it"? But let's look closer.

Much like *Muslim American*, *Asian American* is a tricky category. Asia includes Yemen, India, China, Vietnam, Bangladesh. Asia includes Christians, Muslims, Sikhs, Buddhists. Asia includes people with light skin and blonde hair as well as with kinky dark hair and dark skin. (For more on how the very concept of a continent called "Asia" evolved, see Martin W. Lewis and Kären Wigen's seminal work *The Myth of Continents*.) More importantly for our discussion, the term *Asian American* glosses over the radically different histories that led various Asians to the shores of the United States. The "model minority" story takes a historical fact—that the US government encouraged *certain* Asians, recruited them even, to migrate—and presents it as some kind of innate fact about Asian aptitudes and skills. In 1965, immigration legislation threw the doors wide open to technically skilled, professional Asian migrants as the United States, in deep competition with the USSR during the Cold War, sought the brightest minds from around the world to help build roads, spaceships, airplanes, and more. It's not that "Asians are good at math": it's that, at a particular moment in history, the United States went *looking for* Asians who were good at math. And yes, these migrants certainly *did* achieve the American dream, becoming doctors and engineers. After all, that's what they were brought here to do.

But as the Nigerian writer Chimamanda Ngozi Adichie says, "The problem with stereotypes is not that they are false; it's that they are incomplete."[17] The model minority stereotype of Asian Americans is incomplete because it leaves out the countless migrants who came to the United States from war-torn Vietnam or Laos. (Many of them came as refugees, settling in the United States only to experience deep poverty and become embedded in urban areas rife with gang- and drug-related violence.) It leaves out scores of undocumented South Asian workers in the service sector, workers who—off the books—wash dishes or work as drivers and often struggle to give their children a higher education. It leaves out the history of California, where Asians arrived in droves in the nineteenth and early twentieth century to face segregated schools and laws that prevented them from marrying whites. So, when the model-minority myth proclaims with great confidence that "Asians have made it" in America, it excludes Asians who have been systematically prevented from "making it." Furthermore, such success stories are held up as if to say, "See? Asians made it in this country. Why can't *they*?" The model-minority trope serves as a tool to chastise those people of color who haven't experienced the upward mobility of so-called Asians. It is used to deny the fact of American racism.

As such, the Muslim American success story is similarly problematic. Having US citizenship or an American accent, being white (or white-passing), or having a privileged class status indelibly mitigates how one experiences anti-Muslim sentiment. Yet certain Muslims get to speak prominently about Islamophobia.[18] This might be why Ameena Jandali, founder of the Islamic Networks cultural literacy group, speaking at an Islamic convention, asked people who don't have an American accent to avoid doing media interviews. "Let someone else do it." Such a statement leaves intact a xenophobic intolerance for foreign accents, paving the way for only *certain* Muslims to speak.

THE POLITICS OF RESPECTABILITY

What becomes clear when we study the story of race in America is that when oppressed people portray themselves as moral, upstanding, or worthy of respect, it doesn't actually fight oppression. Take, for instance, responses to the spate of police killings of black people. In the wake of any one of these murders, many will point to the fact that the victim was a veteran, a loving father, or a diligent worker. When Kenneth Chamberlain Sr. was murdered by police after accidentally pushing the call button on his LifeAid system, many pointed to his status as a veteran as a way to drum up sympathy and support. When Philando Castile was murdered in Minnesota, people were quick to point out that he was loved by the schoolchildren he worked with. Each of these claims is a supreme distraction from the *true* issue at hand: the troubling relationship between racist violence and law enforcement.

This, then, is the danger of Islamophilia, of the "good Muslim" trope. It leaves intact the very foundation of anti-Muslim sentiment. In the American racial landscape, terms like *diversity* and *multiculturalism* have been defanged. They've been emptied of any critical content. All too often, they no longer engage with the root causes of oppression and inequality. Instead, diversity has become a box we check, confirming that certain minorities are included in upper ranks, in advertisements, in films. But a *re*-politicizing of diversity would serve us better, for, as Angela Davis tells us, "A multiculturalism that does not acknowledge the *political* character of culture will not . . . lead toward the dismantling of racist, sexist, homophobic, and economically exploitative institutions."[19]

We must avoid expending our energy on including "minorities" in spaces that are available to only a few. Malcolm X reminds us that "sitting at the table doesn't make you a diner"; rather than trying to get a seat at a very exclusive table, we must begin to ask how we can abolish such spaces of exclusion to begin with.

5

CULTURE TALK AS ISLAMODIVERSION

I hope, when we stand up to those who oppress our communities, that Allah accepts from us that as a form of jihad, that we are struggling against tyrants and rulers not only abroad in the Middle East or the other side of the world, but here in the United States of America, where you have fascists and white supremacists and Islamophobes reigning in the White House.

Linda Sarsour, addressing an audience of Muslim Americans at an Islamic convention, sparked outrage with her words.[1] Was she calling for an insurgency? For holy war? For violence against the state? Media pieces expressed fear that Sarsour was calling for an armed insurrection. The kerfuffle even prompted a tweet from Donald Trump Jr., who retweeted a Fox News piece about Sarsour, asking, "Who in the @DNC will denounce this activist and democrat leader calling for Jihad again[st] Trump?"

JIHAD AND OTHER TIRED EXPLANATIONS

Liberals were exasperated: Didn't people know the true meaning of *jihad*? The word simply means "struggle": struggle to improve the world or one's own community, struggle against an unjust tyrant, struggle against oppression. A Muslim can wage jihad by speaking truth, by rejecting oppression, or (yes, in certain cases) through armed struggle.

For over a decade, Muslim spokespeople have been tirelessly explaining jihad's meaning to the public. At cultural-awareness events on college campuses, at interfaith panels, and in earnest op-eds, they have been consistently, patiently reminding America that *jihad* does *not* mean "holy war." *National Geographic* and CNN have published features trying to correct the widespread misunderstanding of *jihad*; popular books by Muslim authors have been devoted to the subject.[2] The Council on American-Islamic Relations (CAIR) took out a series of billboard-sized public transportation ads to tackle the misunderstanding directly. Each ad featured a Muslim American with a caption like "My jihad is to build bridges through friendship," or "My jihad is to stay fit despite my busy schedule." CAIR's campaign was part of a much larger brouhaha that came to be known as the "billboard wars." Pamela Geller, who had previously spearheaded the movement against the Islamic center near Ground Zero, had taken out several ads on city buses asking people to side with "civilized man" rather than the "savage" in order to "defeat jihad." CAIR's campaign was an attempt to respond to Geller's deeply hostile one.

Jihad isn't the only grossly mischaracterized concept Muslim spokespeople have actively explained to the non-Muslim public. Indeed, Muslims have long been engaged in trying to debunk misunderstandings about Islam. Without fail, imams repeat this Qur'anic verse in sermons any time a Muslim commits an act of terrorism: "Whoever kills an innocent being, it shall be as if he had killed all of mankind. And whosoever saves the life of one, it shall be as if he had saved all of mankind." This is partly intended to remind congregants to condemn such violence—but it is also a message to the public that Islam is not an inherently violent faith.

So if Muslim leaders and spokespeople have been repeating, over and over again, these condemnations of terrorism, these reminders of what Islamic principles are, why haven't they "taken"? How come no one is listening?

The short answer is that it doesn't *matter* what *jihad* actually means.

A more earnest answer has to do with the ways we fundamentally misunderstand racism, that we regard it as a matter of prejudice and ignorance. Early in the semester, I ask my students to jot down a definition of racism. They inevitably write things like "disliking people of another race" or "having misperceptions about minorities" or "thinking your own race is superior." Notice that each of these definitions suggest racism is a matter of an individual's *personal* persuasions. They believe, as do many Americans, that racism rests in one's heart and mind. Rarely, if ever, do they mention histories of colonialism and enslavement— histories that are *at the core* of racism. Rarely do their definitions talk about the relative advantage certain groups are given in comparison to others—on the job market, in routine traffic stops, or in their exposure to toxic drinking water. In other words, the conventional wisdom, reflected in my students' responses, is to regard racism as a matter of *attitudes* rather than a matter of *systems*.

Now take anthropologists Roger Sanjek and Steven Gregory's definition: "Race is the framework of ranked categories segmenting the human population that was developed by Western Europeans following their global expansion."[3] I find this definition especially helpful, as it makes clear that ra*cism* has always been connected to the process of colonialism. The history of race isn't about how we've been divided up based upon color or hair texture. Far from it. Race has instead been a way to deem certain people fit to rule and others worthy of enslavement, military occupation, or elimination. Colonialism, warfare, and chattel slavery each required neat categories of humans who were considered fit to be colonized, invaded, or enslaved. The belief that humans could be biologically grouped into such categories is, in short, the story of race.

The racism we regard as a matter of attitudes, prejudices, and misunderstandings is actually a matter of how wealth accumulates over generations.[4] We cannot talk about anti-black racism without understanding how countless elite universities, insurance companies, banks, and apparel retailers wouldn't exist today were it not for their early involvement in the slave system.[5] We cannot tell the story of Native Americans without discussing the US government's unilateral violation of treaties, dispossessing indigenous people of their land. We cannot, quite simply, tell stories of race in America without talking about state violence and power.

If racism were simply attitudinal, located in people's thoughts and opinions, *eliminating* it becomes a matter of changing people's mindsets. It means having more "multicultural days" at schools, more interfaith dialogues at temples and churches, more cultural sensitivity trainings in the workplace. But if we believe, as I do, that racism is *systemic*, about economic systems and state practices, then our whole approach to eliminating it must change. If racism is systemic, fighting it has little to do with changing people's *minds*. Instead, it means redistributing wealth in a way that undoes centuries of injustice. It means ending wars of aggression waged so that countries in the Global North can accumulate wealth. It means unstacking the decks that have been stacked against certain populations for far too long.

ISLAMODIVERSION

Is terrorism committed by Muslims a problem of *Islam*? Is there something inherent in the Islamic faith that drives some of its followers to engage in acts of extremist violence? The question looms large. On an episode of HBO's political talk show *Real Time with Bill Maher*, author and cultural commentator Sam Harris and host Maher agreed that Islamic extremism was a problem rooted in the very religion of Islam.[6] Harris and Maher were disappointed with a "politically correct" America that is afraid to honestly, bluntly call out Islam as backward and oppressive. They echoed what writer Salman Rushdie wrote in an infamous op-ed after 9/11: "Yes, this is about Islam."[7] Actor Ben Affleck, outraged, interrupted them, accusing them of racism against a billion and a half of the world's population. Are Maher, Rushdie, and Harris right? Are extremism, violence, and intolerance natural outgrowths of Islamic theology? Or is Affleck correct—that such a view inappropriately holds all the world's Muslims accountable for the actions of a few bad apples?

Perhaps the answer is more complex. The fact is, while most of the world's Muslims condemn such violence as un-Islamic, people *do* carry out acts of terror in the name of Islam. But what are the roots of this extremist violence the United States has frantically been trying to eliminate? "As a rule," historian Timothy Mitchell tells us, "the most secular regimes in the Middle East have been those most independent of the United States. The more closely a government is allied with the United States, the more Islamic its politics. . . . The United States depends on the support of conservative political regimes, it is often pointed out, and these have tended to rely on religion to justify their power."[8,9] When Western commentators pontificate about the troubling relationship between the religion of Islam and the political violence of Muslim extremists, they often ignore *this* critical context. The version of Islamic practice and interpretation that we now call "fundamentalism" has flourished for multiple, complex reasons. We cannot begin to make sense of them if we omit the crucial role of powerful states themselves. The post–World War II rise of socialist democratic movements in the Arab world, movements that sought to ensure that Arab nations controlled their own wealth and resources rather than being plundered by foreign powers, threatened US oil interests in the region. The story of American involvement in the Middle East reveals just how much effort the United States invested in destabilizing these leftists movements— often by sponsoring the very type of Islam that Bill Maher lambasts as being *anti*-American.

Terrorism experts have spilled much ink on why certain people commit acts of extremist violence. Some of the factors they point to include the person's relationship to his father and mother, exposure to orthodox religious teachings, a childhood in a remote village, even sexual frustration and testosterone. For plenty of terrorism experts, the obvious way to understand and prevent terrorism is to understand an individual's psychology, cultural background, or religious practices.[10] This "culture talk," as anthropologist Mahmood Mamdani calls it, means that people investigate Islam and Muslim *culture* as the source of the problem of terrorism—actively ignoring the *political* realities that give rise to terrorism. Terrorism experts are eager to locate the causes of terrorism within a particular flawed individual or his cultural norms, rather than in larger social systems and political histories. I laughed out loud when I learned that serious military experts thought Saddam Hussein's desire for a nuclear weapon may have stemmed from his treatment by his stepfather.[11]

After 9/11, Columbia University professor Lila Abu-Lughod was approached by several media outlets who asked questions like "Do Muslim women believe x? Are Muslim women y?" We ought to ask ourselves why it was that she was asked about the significance of the burqa in Afghanistan but *not* about the long history of the United States arming and training those forces in Afghanistan who would later be deemed terrorists. "Instead of political and historical explanations," Abu-Lughod says, "experts were being asked to give religio-cultural ones."

Countering Violent Extremism (CVE) initiatives reflect this bias as well. These programs are aimed at preventing terrorism by deterring people who develop extremist views. Under the Obama administration, CVE disproportionately focused on the extremist violence of Muslims, with other religious and ideological extremists receiving less attention. (Trump's administration considered changing the name of CVE to Countering Islamic Extremism, no longer focusing on white-supremacist terrorism at all.) Proponents of CVE argue that the government can predict, based on someone's ideology, the likelihood of their becoming a violent extremist, and argue for a set of interventions that will prevent this turn. The Department of Homeland Security thus spends tens of millions of dollars on "programs that intervene in the radicalization process" and "challenge extremist narratives."[12] This has caused a huge rift in Muslim American communities; those who accept CVE grant money stand accused of cooperating with the devastating effects of state intervention in the lives of Muslims. CVE turns teachers, imams, and social workers into de facto agents of the state.

CVE rests on the assumption that if you topple the belief systems of people who are *likely* to become radicalized, you can thwart terrorism from the roots. According to CVE, one such "ideology" might be a belief among Muslims that the West is at war with Islam. That's right— CVE supporters argue that the belief that the Muslim world is under attack by the West is simply that: a *belief*. Forget the drones that have killed countless children in Yemen and Somalia; forget the unwarranted US invasion of Iraq—nothing to see here. Page after page of CVE literature document how to use the Internet to fight radicalization or introduce positive pathways to young people to deter them from terrorism. Tawfik Hamid, of the Potomac Institute for Policy Studies, argues that young Muslims become attracted to terrorist organizations for such reasons as becoming more religious, wanting status among other Muslims, or desiring revenge on society for perceived injustices.[13] Another CVE suggestion is to recruit, through government funding, "messengers" (i.e., preachers and educators) who will offer "positive" messages to Muslim youth—neutralizing terrorist messaging by introducing Muslims who do not feel alienated by or upset about global circumstances. Leafing through several hundred pages of pro-CVE material, I found myself laughing at the absurdity of the whole program. It talks about anger over imperialist wars and histories of violent colonialism simply a backdrop, turning instead to cultural and ideological interventions to prevent terrorism. A program like CVE could not exist were it not for the widespread understanding that terrorism is motivated by *personal* circumstances rather than *systemic* ones.

Of course, many ordinary Muslims too feel that if people understand their cultures and customs, it will diminish anti-Muslim sentiment. Earnest university students, in an attempt to shift their colleagues' perceptions of Islam, host "hijab days" in which they invite non-Muslim women to try on a headscarf. Many believe this simple act will summon greater understanding of the Muslim experience. It is in this spirit that Muslims across the country host interfaith dialogues: panels whose speakers might include a rabbi, an imam, and a priest, each describing the significance of various elements of faith. Again, such events give Muslims an opportunity to explain themselves, their religious practice, or their culture. Each of these offers the broader public a chance to "know" Islam. Each assumes that Muslims in the West can solve their problems by focusing on attitudes, knowledge, and ideology—rather than political realities.

What happens when we choose to engage in a dialogue about cultural diversity instead of about political facts? What happens when we turn to understanding each other's religions rather than understanding history? I'd like to suggest that there's a deep trade-off, a sacrifice that is made when we engage in culture talk.

I asked my audience at a workshop I was teaching, "How many of you have heard the phrase *Islam is a religion of peace?*" Everyone's hand shot up. It seemed the Muslim PR machine has spread that one-liner far and wide. Then I asked, "How many of you know about the kill list established under the Obama presidency?" This was a list that granted the president powers to assassinate people, even US citizens, without judicial process; it predominantly targeted Muslims. Legal scholars have warned that the kill list signifies a huge overreach of executive power. Not one hand went up. Similarly, many of my undergrads know that Ramadan is a holy month in which observant Muslims fast, but very few know about the material support the United States provides for the Saudi-led war that has devastated the country of Yemen. Yemen is currently suffering the world's largest cholera outbreak as a result.

Culture talk, then, is a diversion. When we should be thinking about the political relationships between Muslim-majority countries and, say, the United States, we instead think about why some Muslim women wear headscarves or the fact that observant Muslims pray five times daily. "Rather than understanding Islamophobia as a series of actions and beliefs that target Muslims and arise from a generic misunderstanding of who Muslims are and what Islam is," writes Stephen Sheehi, Islamophobia is instead an "ideological phenomenon which exists to promote *political and economic* goals, both domestically and abroad."[14]

"Islamodiversion," as Yasser Louati calls it, allows the overblown fear of Muslim terrorists to become a preoccupation, distracting us from real and likely threats. Instead of focusing on imminent hazards—burdensome student-loan debt, increasingly serious climate catastrophes, slashed funding for education and social welfare—Islamophobia leads the public to become obsessed with the threat posed by Muslims. But Iraq War veteran Michael Prysner sums it up best: "The enemy is the system that sends us to war when it's profitable; the enemies are the CEOs who lay us off from our jobs when it's profitable; they're the insurance companies who do not have healthcare when it's profitable; there's banks who take away our homes when it's profitable. Our enemies are not 5,000 miles away. They are right here at home."[15]

But what if it's not just Islamophobes who use Islamodiversion? What if even those who stand in support of Muslims *against* Islamophobia use Islamodiversionary strategies? When this type of discourse is aimed at the lofty goals of dispelling misconceptions, debunking stereotypes, or spreading awareness about who Muslims are, it colonizes space that *could* be spent creating awareness about the political relationships between the so-called Muslim world and the West. I get invited to deliver lectures on the meaning of the hijab or the status of women in Islam (neither of which, by the way, is my area of expertise) *far* more often than I'm invited to speak about the relationship between racism and war.

Barack Obama's 2008 presidential campaign inspired a wave of support among Muslim voters. For many of them, deeply disturbed by the two "Islamophobia terms" they'd experienced under George W. Bush's presidency, an Obama presidency promised hope and change. For instance, on the campaign trail, Obama carefully and accurately pronounced the name of the country Pakistan. This came after a long line of presidents who had butchered the names of Muslim countries, calling them Eye-Ran, Eye-Rack, or Pack-istan. Indeed, Obama's "presidential" diction, sophistication, and multicultural fluency stood in contrast to Bush's oafish, bumbling style. Bush became the butt of liberals' jokes for pronouncing the word *nuclear* "nuculer" and saying things like "misunderestimated" and "we ought to make the pie higher." Obama seemed far more polished and cosmopolitan in comparison to his predecessor.[16]

But what happens when we applaud efforts toward inclusion or cultural awareness and allow our analysis to stop there? Consider the case of Ahmed Mohamed, a fourteen-year-old in Texas who was arrested after showing his teacher a clock he'd built. The teacher thought it was a bomb and promptly had the boy arrested.[17] Mohamed's arrest reflected the widespread anxieties and prejudices of much of the American public. For many who were aghast at the episode of bigotry, it was a relief when President Obama tweeted "Cool clock!" and publicly invited the youth to the White House. In that moment, it seemed that one was either in favor of the teacher, who had good reason to be suspicious of an Arab youth's ticking invention, *or* on the side of Obama, who was standing against this act of racism. But outside of this public debate, some found Obama's gesture deeply hypocritical. A piece in *Gawker*—titled "Obama's Drone Program Probably Would Have Killed Ahmed the Clock Kid"—pointed out that the Obama administration automatically deemed adult Muslim men "combatants" rather than "civilians." In other words, when one of Obama's drones took the life of a Muslim man in a country like Yemen, his death would not be tallied as a civilian death. This is an effective way the state has downplayed the civilian death count. DC-based organizer Darakshan Raja wrote on Facebook about the hypocrisy of the White House invitation, drawing attention to how the Obama administration itself had explicitly singled out Muslim youth not unlike Ahmed Mohamed for policing and monitoring in its Countering Violent Extremism program.

LIBERAL ISLAMOPHOBIA

In fact, the Obama presidency was not a reversal of the Islamophobia of the Bush presidency but a continuation of it. Obama renewed and extended the Patriot Act, continued wholesale the surveillance and profiling of Muslim communities, and kept the racist and illegal prison in Guantanamo Bay open. "The truth is that my foreign policy is actually a return to the traditional bipartisan realistic policy of George Bush's father, of John F. Kennedy, of, in some ways, Ronald Reagan," Obama said. As Deepa Kumar points out, Obama "deployed 30,000 more troops to Afghanistan, expanded the war into Pakistan, tried to bully Iraq into granting an extension of the US occupation (which failed), carried out drone attacks and 'black ops' in Yemen and Somalia and participated in the NATO-led war in Libya."[18] For such critics, Obama's gestures of tolerance and inclusion served as little more than a shroud for his much more pernicious anti-Muslim policies.

In 2016, American voters were again offered a shrouded Islamophobia. With Donald Trump calling for bans on Muslim immigrants and hinting at the creation of a Muslim registry, Hillary Clinton's nods toward inclusion made her the preferable candidate for many Muslim voters. Other Republican candidates addressed the "Muslim issue": Senator Ted Cruz called for more surveillance and policing of Muslims, while Republican candidate Dr. Ben Carson spoke of Islam's fundamental "inconsistency" with American constitutional values. Hillary Clinton responded to such statements, calling them "shameful and contrary to our values." Addressing Muslims, Clinton said, "What you're hearing from Trump and other Republicans is absolutely, unequivocally wrong. It's inconsistent with our values as a nation—a nation which you are helping to build. This is your country, too, and I'm proud to be your fellow American." Clinton, then, drew a line in the sand (as did many voters), designating Islamophobia as the property of Republicans and herself an ally to Muslims.

But Clinton was among those politicians who supported the Iraq War—a decidedly *Islamophobic* stance, as we will see in the following chapter. As Secretary of State, Clinton also signed off on intensifying military intervention in Muslim-majority countries, throwing her head back in a hearty laugh while proclaiming "We came, we saw, he died" of the brutal murder of Libyan leader Gaddafi. Media mogul Haim Saban, who has endorsed racial profiling of Muslims, was one of her top campaign donors. Clinton also voted for the Patriot Act and its reauthorization.

Clinton came under fire for rendering Muslims "instruments" in the fight against terror, saying in the October 9, 2016, presidential debate, "We need American Muslims to be part of our eyes and ears on the front lines." Her statement reinforced the assumption that ordinary Muslims have both a special ability and an extra responsibility to prevent acts of terror. But, writes Ismat Mangla, "American Muslims don't possess some special knowledge of terror attacks. . . . Their citizenship shouldn't come with conditions—it's not contingent on how 'useful' they are in the war on terror."[19] We certainly don't ask white Americans to be our eyes and ears on the battle against mass shootings in suburban schools. In light of such positions, it's peculiar that Clinton was rendered the *pro-Muslim* candidate. Perhaps it was enough for her to take photos with women in hijabs, speak positively of Muslim Americans' contributions, and condemn the Islamophobia of the Trump campaign to erase her more sinister systemic relationship to Muslims.

The histories of Clinton and Obama suggest that we ought to be serious in thinking not just about a bigoted "right-wing" Islamophobia, but also about a *liberal* Islamophobia. "Liberal Islamophobia may be rhetorically gentler," Kumar explains, "but it reserves the right of the US to wage war against 'Islamic terrorism' around the world, with no respect for the right of self-determination by people in the countries it targets. . . . This is the modus operandi of liberal Islamophobia: to roundly reject Islam-bashing—then proceed to institute proposals that target Muslims."[20] Liberal Islamophobes maintain relationships with *certain* Muslims, visit mosques, and wish Muslims a blessed Ramadan, all the while supporting or instituting anti-Muslim policies.

Like Kumar, I find it essential to expose *liberal* Islamophobia and the "good Muslim" trope as thoroughly as we scrutinize the more "obvious," outright bigotry of right-wing Islamophobia. Identifying the rhetorically kinder forms of exclusion is just as crucial as making sense of explicit anti-Muslim hatred. Indeed, the two forms of Islamophobia exist in a delicate balance, intertwined, propping each other up. When George W. Bush was president, he referred to waging "Crusades" against terrorism. This unfortunate turn of phrase revealed an age-old racist Western hostility against the Muslim world. In contrast, Obama's Cairo speech was dedicated to addressing and debunking anti-Muslim stereotypes. Yet just how different were the two figures with regard to the Muslim world? If we don't think critically about such gestures, we risk defeating right-wing Islamophobia only to replace it with its more surreptitious alter ego.

In this chapter, we have seen how Islamophobia, at its core, is systemic. While hate crimes against women in hijabs and vandalism of mosques are certainly Islamophobic, they are but the tip of the iceberg. The actions of powerful state actors give rise to such incidents. (We will consider this dimension more closely in the next chapter.) I have suggested that we need to move away from the idea that Islamophobia is simply a prejudice, embedded in the hearts and minds of individuals. Indeed, this shift would serve Muslim communities well: without it, they will continue to spend undue resources on influencing people's perceptions and awareness about Islam. For example, when I spoke with an Arab American fieldwork contact named Hatem about his decision to leave an organization that was spending too much of its energy on "culture talk," he said to me,

> Mosque-building campaigns are easy to talk about, but what about the hard issues? For instance, George W. Bush killed a million Muslims in Iraq and thousands in Afghanistan, but they have never condemned him. Instead, they invite George W. Bush to their mosques! How can anybody with a conscience do that? You say, thank you, President Bush, for drawing a distinction between good Muslims and bad Muslims? For saying that some of us are okay? For these Muslims, they want to be accepted and appear in the media. And they're willing to pay the price to do that. That price is to ignore war crimes, to legitimize foreign policy! While *we* want to say this war on terror is illegal and we are opposed to it, because of them, the government sees a few Muslims on their side. You know, they see that some Muslims and Arabs are supporting them.

We turn now to the matter of foreign policy.

6

US EMPIRE'S MUSLIM CHEERLEADERS

Amid all the flag-waving, the nationalist fervor, and the growing anti-Arab, anti-Muslim, and anti-immigrant sentiment, Arab, Muslim, and South Asian communities have engaged in a strategic adaptation, a cultural and political accommodation. Many of them have seized the American flag as their own, waving it more fervently, and indeed, preemptively, embracing the flag as a shield.
—Muneer Ahmad[1]

At the 2016 Democratic National Convention (DNC) in Philadelphia, the party's energies were directed against one figure: Donald Trump. Trump's anti-Muslim posturing, including ominous threats to ban all Muslims from entering the country and to murder the families of terrorists, made him an easy target for Democrats' outrage.

PATRIOTISM AS MILITARISM

In a show of defiance, one of the main speakers at the DNC was a man named Khizr Khan. Khan, a Muslim man whose son had died fighting in the US war in Iraq, took the podium and delivered what was arguably the climactic address of the convention, with an outright challenge to Donald Trump:

Hillary Clinton was right when she called my son "the best of America." If it was up to Donald Trump, he never would have been in

America. Donald Trump consistently smears the character of Muslims. He disrespects other minorities, women, judges, even his own party leadership. He vows to build walls and ban us from this country. Donald Trump, you're asking Americans to trust you with their future. Let me ask you: have you even read the United States Constitution? I will gladly lend you my copy. [He pulls it out.] In this document, look for the words "liberty" and "equal protection of law." Have you ever been to Arlington Cemetery? Go look at the graves of brave patriots who died defending the United States of America. You will see all faiths, genders, and ethnicities. You have sacrificed nothing and no one. We cannot solve our problems by building walls, sowing division. We are stronger together. And we will keep getting stronger when Hillary Clinton becomes our president. In conclusion, I ask every patriotic American, all Muslim immigrants, and all immigrants to not take this election lightly. This is a historic election, and I request to honor the sacrifice of my son—and on Election Day, take the time to get out and vote.[2]

Raucous applause ensued. Khan became the "star" of the DNC. His speech that night embodied a quintessential patriotism, reminding the audience of a son perished in war, brandishing a copy of the Constitution as an affront to Trump. He was the Democratic Party's archetypical model Muslim.

We have spoken of markers of legitimacy such as class, profession, and educational status. That July evening, Khan's speech positioned the loss of his son in a US war as a marker of legitimacy for American Muslims, issuing a reminder that Muslims too serve in the US war machine. This might explain the roaring applause. Service in the Iraq war has become another marker of legitimacy; support for the armed forces and their military incursions is a baseline credential for Muslims to prove their worth. Think, for instance, about how Republican senator John McCain opposed Trump's "Muslim ban" for the reason that it would impact Iraqis who had assisted the US military's invasion. Scholar Michelle Sandhoff tells us, "Being included in the military is a powerful indicator that you are seen as a member of the nation and you have the right (and duty) to defend it."[3]

The feeling that Muslims ought not to be discriminated against because of their support for American warfare has a much longer history. In 2008, former Secretary of State Colin Powell appeared on *Meet the*

Press and condemned the anti-Muslim sentiment many Republicans were using to smear Barack Obama as Muslim and therefore un-American. Powell spoke of a photograph he saw in a magazine. "It was a photo essay about troops who are serving in Iraq and Afghanistan," he said.

> And when I saw the picture, it was of a mother in Arlington Cemetery. And she had her head on the headstone of her son's grave. . . . And you could see the writing on the headstone. It gave his awards: Purple Heart, Bronze Star. Showed that he died in Iraq. . . . The very top of the headstone didn't have a Christian cross. It didn't have a Star of David. It had a crescent and a star, of the Islamic faith. And his name was Kareem Rashad Sultan Khan. And he was an American.[4]

For Powell, this Muslim man's death was enough to make him American through and through.

It's worthwhile to consider what it means to use one's support of the US war machine as a marker of legitimacy. Let's take what began in 2003 in Iraq as an example. Even though neither Saddam Hussein nor any Iraqis had anything to do with 9/11, as a predominantly Muslim and Arab country, Iraq was, nebulously, *somehow* guilty of anti-American terrorism. I was a college student in 2003 and had only recently become immersed in studying the politics and history of US–Middle East relations. I saw my peers expressing support for the war in ways that confused and troubled me. I remember sitting in a dorm room with friends, stunned, as I heard a neighbor say, "Do you think any country would let what happened on 9/11 happen to it and *not* need to go to war with someone?" For him, as for countless other Americans, the facts didn't really matter. It was enough to declare war on "them," and "they" were Muslim and Arab enough to deserve it. In fact, the whole war effort relied on such slippages. Some supported the war because it would offer the United States a chance to carry out regime change and dethrone Saddam Hussein, the brutal dictator. It didn't matter to them that the United States supports dictators aplenty, nor that the United States was responsible for Hussein's political career to begin with. Others felt that the war was justified because Hussein had weapons of mass destruction (interesting, given that the United States had helped Iraq develop its chemical-weapons arsenal during its war with Iran in the

1980s). Nor did it matter that Hussein had condemned Al-Qaeda and Islamist terrorism,[5] that he had expressed sorrow and condolences over the events of 9/11, or that he had offered to help the United States fight violent religious extremism.[6]

What *did* matter for countless Americans who supported the war was that Iraq is Arab, Muslim, and (as it was dubbed by George W. Bush) part of an "axis of evil." The journalist and political prisoner Mumia Abu-Jamal reminds us of the racist, colonialist logics that stood behind the Iraq invasion: "One need not look far to find a general likening the Iraq war to 'holy war' against 'unbelievers'; or to hear US military members referring to Arabs/Muslims as 'ragheads,' 'hajjis,' or the Reagan-era colloquialism 'sand niggers.'"[7] Michael Prysner, an Iraq War veteran, echoes Abu-Jamal's argument that the Iraq invasion relied on racism: "I began to hear new words like 'towel head,' 'camel jockey' and—the most disturbing—'sand nigger.' These words did not initially come from my fellow soldiers, but from my superiors—my platoon sergeant, my company first sergeant, my battalion commander. All the way up the chain of command, viciously racist terms were suddenly acceptable."[8] This points to precisely the type of *racial* thought that lay behind the war effort. Look no further than the fact that Bernard Lewis, one of America's most notorious anti-Muslim intellectuals, was present in the Bush administration's September 2001 meetings about just how to craft the "war on terror," including the war effort in Iraq.[9] The result? The public was provided constant reminders that this war was against *them*: a racialized Islamic threat.

The racist division between "civilized" Americans and "uncivilized" Iraqis surfaced most clearly when horrendous abuses were revealed at Abu Ghraib prison. In 2003, disturbing photographs showed American soldiers torturing and sexually abusing Iraqi inmates, leading to much larger revelations of torture in US detention centers (for instance, at Guantanamo Bay). Even when Americans were caught red-handed committing these atrocities at Abu Ghraib, American political discourse revealed a sense of superiority. Consider Michael Barone, writing of the scandal: "Americans hold themselves to high standards, and if others hold us to those standards even while they excuse or ignore the far more evil acts of others—like the mass murders and tortures of Saddam Hussein's regime—that's the price we must pay."[10] For Barone, even Americans' sense of disgust over the military's use of torture at Abu

Ghraib was evidence of American superiority: we're better than them because at least *we* feel bad about torturing them.

THE US THIRST FOR WAR

In 2002, before the war began, writer Arundhati Roy said:

> Weapons inspectors have conflicting reports of the status of Iraq's weapons of mass destruction, and many have said clearly that its arsenal has been dismantled and that it does not have the capacity to build one. However, there is no confusion over the extent and range of America's arsenal of nuclear and chemical weapons. Would the US government welcome weapons inspectors? . . . What if Iraq does have a nuclear weapon? Does that justify a preemptive US strike? The US has the largest arsenal of nuclear weapons in the world and it's the only country in the world to have actually used them on civilian populations. If the US is justified in launching a pre-emptive strike on Iraq, why, then any nuclear power is justified in carrying out a pre-emptive strike on any other. India could attack Pakistan, or the other way around. If the US government develops a distaste for, say, the Indian prime minister, can it just "take him out" with a preemptive strike?[11]

At the time, dissenting voices like Roy's were bludgeoned into silence. The Dixie Chicks, a country-music band, were all but blacklisted for speaking out against the war. Or consider journalist Helen Thomas, who stood to ask Bush a question at a press conference. "Why did you really want to go to war?" she asked. "You have said it wasn't oil. It wasn't Israel. So what was it?" Bush responded by invoking the 9/11 attacks. Thomas rebutted, "They didn't do anything to you, or to our country." Bush responded again with a response about Afghanistan, home to the Taliban and Al-Qaeda. "I'm talking about *Iraq*," Thomas said. In his final response, Bush offered a vague answer about Saddam Hussein's weapons program and dictatorship.[12] Almost two decades later, the United States stands responsible for a war that has left more than a million Iraqis dead—and the number is rising.

But the story hardly starts with the 2003 invasion. Iraq's history is marked by meddling by foreign powers (British and American, primarily)—meddling that involved disrupting democratic movements, establishing dictatorships, and arming unsavory leaders, in large part to enrich the United States (for instance, through the extraction of oil wealth). When the United States was reckoning with the "threat" of Iranian power in the Middle East, Iraq (and Saddam Hussein specifically) had served as a key ally to the United States. Hussein received handy support, even when acting as a brutal dictator, when he was protecting US interests in the region. Eventually, though, he would stop acting on behalf of the United States. In 1991, the United States went to war with Iraq after Hussein ordered an invasion of Kuwait. Two separate UN humanitarian coordinators resigned after declaring that the civilian costs of US and British bombing campaigns in Iraq were unconscionable.[13] What followed that war was years of US sanctions that left a whole generation of Iraqis to suffer malnutrition, illness, and poverty. While President Clinton officially issued these sanctions as a punishment for Saddam Hussein, their impact was felt by ordinary Iraqis. When then–Secretary of State Madeleine Albright appeared on a 60 Minutes news segment in 1996, Lesley Stahl asked about the Iraq sanctions, "We have heard that half a million children have died. That's more children than died in Hiroshima. Is the price worth it?" Albright replied, "It is a hard choice, but we think the price is worth it."

My students are stunned to learn of the close relationship that existed between the United States and the very Saddam Hussein who was later dubbed the ultimate threat to US stability. This history—of alliances, destabilizations, sanctions, and invasions—has left an Iraq so devastated, so weakened, that it seems almost natural that a group like ISIS should form. ISIS took hold in the midst of a toppled Iraqi state and the desperation of a population that had lived through far too much trauma. Today many in the United States have some understanding of ISIS as the "bad guy" in the region, but very little historical understanding about how this militant Sunni Muslim group rose to power on the global stage.

Politicians on both sides of the aisle were eager to support the 2003 Iraq invasion: twenty-nine Democratic senators and all but one Republican senator voted for it. This points to a consensus between our political parties when it comes to matters of warfare and foreign policy. Over the nationalistic fervor that swept post-9/11 America, it was difficult to hear the reminders that this invasion stood on shaky ground. It seems a sinister joke that the war effort was initially called Operation Iraqi Liberation—before someone realized the acronym OIL would be in poor taste.

A similar climate had surrounded the US invasion of Afghanistan in 2001. Reeling from the 9/11 attacks, many weren't willing to engage, or capable of engaging, in nuanced, deliberate historical analysis. It wasn't the time to point out that the United States had provided military training, weapons, and over $3 billion to Osama bin Laden and the Afghan *mujahideen* when they were fighting the Soviet Union on behalf of the United States.[14] (Of course, the United States siding with unsavory characters, so long as they were on our side, was made explicit in the words attributed (probably apocryphally) to President Franklin Roosevelt, speaking of the Nicaraguan dictator Anastasio Somoza, whose family's rule the United States supported for some forty years: "He may be a son of a bitch, but he's *our* son of a bitch.") As Sheehi notes, "After it emerged that the Afghan fighters . . . were linked to the events of September 11, 2001, many Americans referred to them as 'Frankenstein monsters'—creations of the US government that ultimately turned on their creator in a catastrophic way."[15]

To date, the war in Afghanistan is the longest the United States has waged, and it shows no signs of ending. In fact, in 2017, Donald Trump announced that he was sending more ground troops—despite having tweeted in 2013: "Let's get out of Afghanistan. Our troops are being killed by Afghanis and we waste billions there. Nonsense! Rebuild the USA."[16] Trump's furthering the Afghan war effort after promising to end it hardly came as a surprise. After all, many who had opposed George W. Bush because of his invasion of Afghanistan eagerly threw their support behind Barack Obama, expecting that he, too, would end it. But Obama also intensified the war effort in Afghanistan. Afghanistan's devastation would seem guaranteed, regardless of the figure in the White House.

The "war on terror" has been marked by pyrrhic victories: Saddam Hussein was ousted, but ISIS rose in his place. Osama bin Laden was murdered, but that hardly heralded the end of Islamist terrorism. In fact, there were 62 terrorist incidents in Afghanistan in the nine years leading up to the war, and 2,358 in the nine years after. In Iraq, the nine years before the war saw 111 terrorist incidents; the nine years after saw 6,003. "If this is an effective campaign," writes Heather Brown, "one can only imagine what ineffectiveness would look like."[17]

Khizr Khan gaining legitimacy and arousing a standing ovation for reminding the public that his son proudly served in this war—an illegal, devastating war—thus rests upon some gruesome logic. (It's worth noting that Khan has, in other interviews, been highly critical of US military policy in Muslim-majority countries. This didn't garner as much press time as his jingoistic display at the DNC.)

Khan, as a figure of a pro-military Muslim American, reminded me of an experience of my own in the months following September 11. A teacher of mine reached out to me to offer kind words of support. She was worried about me, she said, given the anti-Muslim climate after 9/11. I responded, telling her that, though I felt safe, I was troubled by the looming threat of the American invasion of Afghanistan. She responded curtly, "I suppose you live in this country, so you're entitled to your opinion." It was clear: she was ready to lend her support and tolerance to Muslims, but this support came with conditions. When it came to the question of politics, foreign policy, and state-sanctioned anti-Muslim action, she fell neatly in line with the bipartisan project of Islamophobia.

This is what is expected of Muslims who wish to be incorporated into the nation as Americans: unflappable support for the nation's project of empire. For Muslims vying for legitimacy (and, in the case of Khan, redeemed by the Democratic Party), they would have to declare their allegiance to the US military machine, even in its most troubling iterations.

IMPERIALISM

"Jesus!" exlaimed a student in my course Race and Islam in the United States, during a unit on proxy warfare during the Cold War. "Just how many dictators has the USA supported that it eventually ends up assassinating?" This student, Josiah, was genuinely exasperated, as are many of the students who walk through my classroom doors, at what had been left out of his history lessons. The extent of the United States' role as a global superpower is often lost. "Most Americans," writes Chalmers Johnson,

are probably unaware of how Washington exercises its global hege-
mony, since so much of this activity takes place either in relative
secrecy under comforting rubrics. Many may, as a start, find it hard
to believe that our place in the world even adds up to an empire. But
only when we come to see our country as both profiting from and
trapped within the structures of an empire of its own making will it
be possible for us to explain many elements of the world that otherwise perplex us.[18]

Perhaps the imperialistic and colonial workings of the United States
are unknown to the average American because they are often hidden
from view, "well below the sight lines of the American public."[19] Junaid
Rana speaks of an "American empire that, via its chameleonlike charac-
teristics, is able to hide elements of its domination in plain sight."[20]

In fact, most of my students aren't taught to any appropriate degree
about the history of imperialism at all—be it the empires of Belgium,
Great Britain, and France or the imperialist domination exercised by
the United States over much of the world. They may have read a Mark
Twain novel in high school, but they don't know that Twain was a vocal
leader of the anti-imperialist movement or that he roundly condemned
the US military occupation of the Philippines. (Truth be told, they often
don't know about the United States' gruesome involvement in the Philippines to begin with.) My students—many of them studious, conscientious learners—don't know about the hands and feet that were severed
in the Congo as part of Belgium's enrichment from Congolese rubber
plantations. Many of them don't know about the relatively recent history of South African colonialism; I remember being absolutely stunned
when *no one* in a class of thirty-five undergraduate students could tell
me who Nelson Mandela was. "Dealing with the dark, seamy side of US
involvement in global affairs has never been easy for the citizens of the
United States," anthropologist Lesley Gill tells us, "because of the widespread amnesia about twentieth-century US empire building. A broad
cross-section of Americans like to think of their country as a land of
freedom, a beacon to the oppressed, an exemplary democracy, and
most recently, a righteous crusader against global terrorism."[21]

So, for the benefit of all the victims of American history lessons,
allow me to state the patently obvious: imperialism is *never* a gentle or
kind process. When powerful nations exert political, economic, or military influence over others, it is by definition an act of violence. Imperi-

alism is always, fundamentally, a matter of producing wealth, profit, for an elite. The US's support for dictatorships in Latin America was profitable for the United Fruit Company. British control over Iran generated enormous profits for British Petroleum (BP). Belgium's colonialism in the Congo led to a flourishing rubber trade—fueled by violence against the native Congolese. France vastly enriched its wealth through the slave trade and sugar industry in Haiti. The list goes on.

In fact, imperialism is so brutal that it could *hardly* exist if it presented itself in honest terms. Instead, the people of the United States, Britain, and France are offered a *legitimizing rationale*, a justification for their nations' actions around the world. For imperialism to go forward, ordinary people must accept that these actions better the world, uplift a broken or downtrodden population, or spread positive values like democracy. An imperialist power can hardly proclaim itself openly in search of wealth and riches at the expense of the lives of men, women, and children. This is why British poet Rudyard Kipling wrote of imperialism as "the white man's burden." He saw it as a unique duty for Europeans to civilize and uplift the "savages" of Africa and India. This is why the US government speaks of bringing *democracy* to Iraq or Afghanistan, rather than enriching mercenary armies and securing oil contracts. This is why it spoke of supporting "freedom fighters" in the 1980s in Nicaragua, all the while financing the Nicaraguan *contras*, who were right-wing terrorists. Napoleon charged into Egypt claiming he would save Egyptians from being hung by their own leaders. And when King Leopold embarked on his process of subjugating the Congo to his rule, he spoke of it not as a profit-making venture but as a way to uplift Africans.

In this way, colonizing forces justify their plunder. They have carefully masked it with a sheath of salvation, advancement, liberation, democracy, even feminism. For European colonialism, it was a *mission civilisatrice*—a civilizing mission. It was this that prompted Aimé Césaire to write:

> Between the colonizer and the colonized there is room only for forced labor, intimidation, pressure, the police, taxation, theft, rape, compulsory crops, contempt, mistrust, arrogance, self-complacency, swinishness, brainless elites, degraded masses. . . . They talk to me about progress, about "achievements," diseases cured, improved standards of living. *I* am talking about societies drained of their es-

sence, cultures trampled underfoot, institutions undermined, lands confiscated, religions smashed, magnificent artistic creations destroyed, extraordinary possibilities wiped out.[22]

Today the United States stands as an imperialist power, with a military budget as large as those of the next seven countries *combined*. America's military apparatus explicitly relies on colonialism, with people from places like Guam and American Samoa serving in the armed forces in spite of not being legal citizens. There are hundreds of US military bases scattered in all corners of the world. Yet while the fact of American empire seems so obvious, it remains obscured. Enseng Ho speaks of American empire as hiding in plain sight:

> While previous empires dominated their colonies with pomp and ceremony, the American invention of "extraterritoriality" formalizes the idea that Americans are not really present . . . two priorities at least are clear for the US government: internal securitization of the US population itself, and an increased investment in methodologies of invisibility abroad. Remote control bombers fly ever higher out of sight, while military advisors disappear into the Filipino jungles, Yemeni mountains, and Georgian gorges. As well, security, military, and colonial functions are farmed out to private companies, removing them from political oversight.[23]

Understanding these legitimizing rationales may help us understand why the United States has gotten away with violence scot-free while its mercenary army, Blackwater, makes skyrocketing profits despite massacring Iraqi civilians. (Read Jeremy Scahill's terrific book *Blackwater: The Rise of the World's Most Powerful Mercenary Army* on the subject.[24]) It might help us understand why the United States armed and trained death squads, with the specific intent to quash democratic uprisings in Latin America, at a military school in Fort Benning, Georgia. (Read Lesley Gill's *The School of the Americas: Military Training and Political Violence in the Americas*.) Chalmers Johnson writes about the huge arms industry, military disasters, and terrorist attacks against the United States as evidence of "a 21st-century crisis in America's informal empire, an empire based on the projection of military power to every corner of the world and on the use of American capital and markets to force global economic integration on our terms, at whatever cost to others."[25] The legitimizing rationale for US empire, what Jean Bricmont calls humanitarian imperialism, masks all of this. "Every relationship of domination is, in the last analysis, military, and always needs an ideology as justification. The ideology of our times . . . is a certain discourse on human rights and democracy. . . . This discourse justifies Western interventions in the Third World in the name of the defense of democracy and human rights."[26]

This elementary understanding of imperialism ought to be the backbone for any conversation about Islamophobia. In 2001, many in the United States saw themselves as *unique* victims and 9/11 as an unprecedented type of tragedy. A veritable industry of mourning 9/11 cropped up, with memorial coins and pins and flags for purchase. Phrases like "we will never forget" branded the events as a supreme catastrophe. Of course, to any student of history, 9/11 was hardly unique in scope or scale: in fact, the date 9/11 itself stands as a stark reminder of American involvement in Chile's 1973 coup, in which leftist leader Salvador Allende was replaced by a right-wing dictator, Augusto Pinochet. Lesley Gill reminds us that "the events in the United States and in Chile, so different in many ways, shared two important features: the deaths of thousands of civilians and the involvement of the United States in training the terrorists."[27] But historical fact wasn't guiding US social consciousness in late 2001. Instead, what swept the nation was something conservative radio host Glenn Beck called "the spirit of 9/12." This was a spirit of ferocious jingoism, when American flags festooned storefronts and car antennas and front porches. The very concept of the homeland became something Americans were expected to guard fiercely. In this context, warfare seemed to many to be the most obvious response.

WHY THEY HATE US

This was the moment when President Bush stood up and said of the attackers, "They hate our freedoms."[28] This statement, pregnant with meaning, rendered those of *us* in the United States uniquely free, and *them* somehow encumbered, in chains. In the US imagination, countries like Iraq, Afghanistan, Pakistan, and Sudan each stand in neat contradistinction to the liberties *we* enjoy. It's *over there* that people are executed for petty crimes. It's *over there* that women deal with extraordinary oppression. It's *over there* that minorities don't enjoy any rights, liberties, or inclusion. This worldview stands firm, even in the face of ample evidence contradicting it. For example, in 2011, the state of Georgia executed a man named Troy Davis for murder *even after* the witnesses in his trial admitted to providing false testimony and the actual murderer confessed to the crime. I brought a discussion of the Davis execution to my students at the time; our class was studying the relationships between law, race, and justice. "Okay, so maybe he didn't do the murder," said Becky. "But come on, he was in prison. On death row. He must have done *something*." It was beyond Becky's imagination that the justice system in the United States could be so deeply flawed as to knowingly execute an innocent man. "We have due process. We're not, like, some Third World country," she added.

If, as Becky believes, America is the land of freedom, rights, and equality, the United States would then have to at least gesture toward equality for women. This means trouble for us: after all, there are places in the United States where women are required by law to get permission from a rapist before getting an abortion.[29] It means that the criminal justice system would have to treat all equally. More trouble, for black people are arrested, incarcerated, and executed at much higher rates than white people for the very same crimes.[30] It means, critically, that the United States couldn't be marked by deep bigotry, intolerance, or racial hatred. In other words, in order to maintain the legitimizing rationale for imperialism, the nation would have to find some way to "include" Muslims. Anti-Muslim bigotry might in fact *tarnish* the United States' claims to being exceptional. If the United States is to continue to spend billions on a war that it argues is against antidemocratic, repressive, hateful forces, then it must show that it is none of those things.

The war on terror is hardly the first time the United States' purported goals abroad have clashed with domestic events. Think about anti-imperialist athlete Muhammad Ali's famous rejection of military service:

> Why should I put on a uniform and go ten thousand miles from home and drop bombs and bullets on Brown people in Vietnam while so-called Negro people in Louisville are treated like dogs and denied simple human rights? I'm not going 10,000 miles from home

to help murder and burn another poor nation simply to continue the domination of white slave masters over the darker people the world over. This is the day when such evils must come to an end. I have been warned that to take such a stand would cost me millions of dollars. But I have said it once and I will say it again: the real enemy of my people is here. . . . If I thought the war was going to bring freedom and equality to 22 million of my people, they wouldn't have to draft me. I'd join tomorrow. I have nothing to lose by standing up for my beliefs. So I'll go to jail. So what? We've been in jail for 400 years.[31]

How could the United States claim to be liberating the Vietnamese when its own black citizens were denied access to drinking fountains, colleges, and seats on buses?

In the early decades of the 1900s, the eugenics movement was gaining popularity in the United States. Thousands of eugenicists believed that forced sterilization would prevent "unfit" mothers from having children. Eugenicists sought to prohibit intermarriage and interbreeding with "feeble races" in order to "purify" American society. Yet during World War II, the United States took an overt stand *against* the eugenics of Hitler and the German Nazi Party. What a hypocrisy it would have been for the United States to oppose *their* eugenics while a similar movement swept the land back home. This contradiction needed to be resolved. Indeed, the American eugenics movement did lose steam after World War II.

WHAT "GOOD MUSLIMS" DO

In more recent times, if the war against Islamist terrorism is to hold water, intolerance and bigotry must be seen as *their* problem, not ours. The *enemies* are the ones who are intolerant, parochial, and narrow— not us. On the contrary, the United States must prove itself inclusive of its multiracial, multiethnic national body. This is a large part of why the figure of the "good Muslim" is so critical. Their inclusion is part of the legitimizing rationale for US empire:[32]

Thus, the war on terrorism is *not* simply a war on Muslims, and it is not a holy war. To the contrary, it largely attains legitimacy by presuming and relying on the existence of a category of good Muslims, both within the United States and abroad. The United States of the twenty-first century maintains an identity as a multicultural, (neo)liberal and tolerant state. . . . Perhaps more importantly, the good Muslim category provides a means for Muslims both inside and outside of the United States to support the United States' . . . attempts to fight the war on terrorism, thus reinforcing the war's legitimacy.[33]

There are commentators from Muslim backgrounds who have made their whole careers by simultaneously cheerleading for US imperialism and condemning Muslims' backwardness (for instance, Ayaan Hirsi Ali, Irshad Manji, and Fareed Zakaria).[34]

Marking certain Muslims "good" is certainly not a new tactic. (Mamdani's book *Good Muslim, Bad Muslim: America, the Cold War, and the Roots of Terror* is especially edifying on this topic.) Yet it has taken on a new significance since 9/11 and even more so during the Trump presidency. Declaring that "Islam is a religion of peace" or that "Muslims condemn terror" leaves out a big part of the story. "Liberal Islamophobia," writes Deepa Kumar, "acknowledges that there are good Muslims—those who cooperate with the goals of empire."[35] Arun Kundnani agrees in his book *The Muslims Are Coming!*, telling us, "The liberal caveat is that Muslims are acceptable when depoliticized: they should be silent about politics, particularly US foreign policy and the domestic national security system, and not embrace an alien ideology that removes them from the liberal norm."[36] Through images of Muslims waving American flags, offering their children as tribute to the war machine, or signing up as eager supporters of the fight against Islamic terrorism, the West can celebrate, incorporate, and tolerate *certain* Muslims without ever drawing into question its imperialist project.

Consider a billboard that appeared on the side of a major highway near Chicago. It read, "Hey ISIS—You suck! From, American Muslims." I doubt the billboard was *actually* directed at ISIS, unless there's a covert ISIS cell somewhere off I-90 in Chicago. Instead, it was a defensive act. The billboard message was directed to white Americans by Muslims who are often unfairly asked to "condemn terrorism," as if that's somehow their condemnation to make. Condemning ISIS is ostensibly much safer than condemning US foreign policy. Perhaps for good reason; Corey Robin reminds us that, throughout history, "immigrants who voice strong opinions on questions of foreign policy or politics have also attracted unwanted attention to themselves."[37]

As we saw in chapter 5, without fail, Muslim sermons, panel discussions, and community events included a condemnation of ISIS, terrorism, or violence against civilians. I even attended an Eid sermon in Chicago in which the *khatib* delivered a sermon devoted entirely to condemning the horrors committed by ISIS. I was saddened to see these hundreds of Muslim congregants gathered to celebrate one of the biggest Muslim holidays instead subjected to a lecture condemning a group with which they have no connection. In fact, Muslims across the West have led, organized, and filled the streets in marches against terrorism (for instance, in Germany and Spain in 2017). In other words, Muslims *have* condemned terror.

There's a slippery slope between "condemning terrorism" in these ways and being an implicit advocate for the US war on terror. After all, the latter means implicit support for war efforts such as the ones in Afghanistan and Iraq. It also means supporting the domestic processes of surveillance and policing of Muslim communities. Consider the CVE program discussed in previous chapters, which saw many Muslims themselves—including imams, social workers, and teachers—assisting the state in its surveillance and policing of Muslims. As Sahar Aziz has said, CVE became "a guise for deputizing well-intentioned Muslim leaders to gather intelligence on their constituents that places their civil liberties at risk."[38] In trying to prove oneself a good Muslim, one must essentially become a willing participant in Islamophobia itself.

But Islamophobia will not be defeated by recruiting certain Muslims to carry out racialized, ineffective policing against their own communities. Nor will terrorism be defeated by sending Muslim American soldiers out to fight and die in wars of aggression in Muslim-majority countries. The goal of principled antiracism is never to incorporate "minorities" into an existing power structure. Asking to be integrated into the top of a racial hierarchy doesn't dismantle the racial hierarchy; it leaves it intact. Principled antiracism means seeking to abolish the very *roots* of imperialism and racism. Otherwise, we will be satisfied when arms dealers like Lockheed Martin set up Friday prayer spaces for their employees rather than thinking about the troubling role of the arms industry in the American economy.

There is a vast difference between pointing to Muslims who serve faithfully in the US military and pointing to the transgressions of the military itself. For a society that is so shamefully accustomed to racism and militarism, *these* critiques are far harder to make. If we're not careful, US empire will have us celebrating the inclusion of all races, gender identities, and religions in its sinister project of global power.

7

BEYOND TRUMP

On November 9, 2016, I woke up to a bevy of text messages expressing shock and disappointment at the results of the presidential election. On campus, I found coworkers in tears, hugging each other in disbelief. A steady stream of students appeared in my office that day, many of them sobbing. "This is not America," some said, echoing a sentiment that swept liberal pockets of the nation. One white student whose parents were Trump supporters collapsed in my arms, weeping, "I have no family anymore." In one of my classes, a Muslim student wearing a hijab interrupted my lecture to say, "I just want anyone in this room to know, if you voted for Trump, you're racist. It's that simple." In another class, a Bangladeshi American student wept openly in the middle of class. "I never believed my parents when they told me how much this country hated us. But I believe them now." It was by far the most dramatic day at work I'd ever had. What followed over the course of Trump's years in office was a wide-ranging and self-proclaimed "resistance." Celebrities, establishment Democrats,[1] and even some disgruntled Republicans would join this resistance movement, seeing in Trump a betrayal of the America they so cherished.

Trump's election came as a surprise to many. I, like many Americans, had been preparing for the inevitability of a Hillary Clinton presidency. She was expected to defeat Trump in the 2016 election. Her campaign leaned on her identity as a woman to gain support from liberal voters. With celebrities like Beyoncé, Lady Gaga, and Alyssa Milano hailing her nomination as a momentous step forward for gender equality, the public also began to accept this view. Emily Bazelon wrote in the *New York Times*, "Mrs. Clinton owned her feminism. She sounded like the first woman running for president, defending other women—our autonomy and our control of our bodies."[2] Yet for those who had paid close attention to Clinton's years as New York senator and Secretary of State, this was a perverse brand of feminism indeed. As Obama's Secretary of State, Clinton oversaw a military incursion to overthrow the Libyan leader Muammar Gaddafi that would become a stain on the Obama presidency. In Haiti, Clinton was a key architect of antidemocratic economic and political decisions that devastated ordinary Haitians.[3] And as a board member of Walmart, her support for the company's anti-union efforts and practices of gender discrimination became clear.[4] For those who understood this history, the celebration of her gender identity was a grand distraction from the substance of her politics. A comic strip circulated featuring a Muslim couple bombarded by missiles. In it, the man turns to the hijab-clad woman and says, "They say the next one will be sent by a woman," to which she responds, "really makes you feel like part of history." Such critiques, however, were of little concern to Clinton's feminist fan base. In fact, many of them saw such criticism itself as a form of sexism. (We will return to the concept of "imperialist feminism" later in this chapter.) So upsetting was the prospect of a Clinton presidency to many who knew this history that in 2016, when the Democratic National Convention was held in Philadelphia, thousands of protestors took to the streets. The march consisted of leftists and Black Lives Matter supporters who felt compelled to resist the Democratic Party, just as they would resist the Trump presidency in the coming years.

Regardless of whether Donald Trump or Hillary Clinton won the 2016 election, the United States would see at its helm a leader who would expand US war-making, create the conditions that lead to migration, expand the militarized system of policing, and pass economic policy widening the gap between rich and poor. Trump's presidency certainly did so. On the day of Trump's inauguration, the White House's webpages on climate change, civil rights, and LGBT issues were taken down.[5] His presidency empowered white supremacists and xenophobes to go public with their views. In 2017, a white nationalist rally was held in Charlottesville, Virginia, its participants marching through the streets yelling Nazi chants. One of the anti-racist protestors who gathered to speak against this rally was killed in the violence that unfolded.[6] Hate crimes against Muslims and Jews spiked. Donald Trump pardoned sheriff Joe Arpaio, who had been found guilty of racially profiling Latinx people, forcing them to wear pink underwear while incarcerated in overheated outdoor tents.[7] And while the Ku Klux Klan has endorsed other US presidents, Trump made no moves to renounce their endorsement of him.

As Trump's presidential campaign had made clear, Islamophobia would be a cornerstone of his presidency. It came as little surprise when he passed Executive Order 13769, the "Muslim ban." In 2017, Donald Trump retweeted videos from the ultraright group Britain First that falsely depicted Muslim violence against Europeans. When asked about the fake videos, Trump's press secretary Sarah Huckabee Sanders said, "Look, whether or not it's a real video, the threat is real. And that is what the president is focused on, is dealing with those threats. And those are real, no matter how you look at it."[8] Trump's demagogic Islamophobia would inspire a gunman in New Zealand to open fire at a mosque, killing seventy-seven Muslim worshippers.[9]

However, despite his brazen bigotry, Trump was hardly an *anomaly* in the American political system. We cannot understand the Islamophobic Trump presidency without first understanding the context that produced it, especially the elements outside the Republican Party. In an especially bizarre twist, we will see how many figures who crafted policies of war-making, militarized policing, and economic injustice would later brand themselves part of an anti-Trump resistance. The "Trump Syndrome," in which critics of Donald Trump regard him as a freakish outlier in American politics, would impact the 2020 presidential race between Biden/Harris and Trump/Pence. My hope is that this chapter clarifies what it means to have a politics of substance rather than form, to understand Donald Trump not as an orange-hued Twitter bully who has betrayed American values but rather as another in a series of US presidents who have expanded American militarism, authoritarianism, and state repression.

PRESIDENT TRUMP IN CONTEXT

I was attending a protest in Philadelphia shortly after the inauguration of Donald Trump. It was not an anti-Trump protest, nor was it a pro–Hillary Clinton march. People were not wearing the pink hats that dotted the crowds at the famous "women's marches" that would take place two months later. At this protest, Philadelphians (most of them black and native to Philly) had gathered to demonstrate against the long record of anti-black police brutality in the city of Philadelphia. I stood next to a young black man who held a sign that said, on one side, "Demilitarize the police" and on the other, "Who do you protect? Who do you serve?" He said,

> This is *not* about Donald Trump. This isn't about the Republicans. In fact, Philly is a city that's always run by Democrats. So? Has that kept black folks safe from the violence of law enforcement? Has that meant that our schools are well funded? Does that mean that the city isn't being taken over by real estate developers, who gentrify our neighborhoods and make it impossible for us to afford our homes? White people are so shocked that Donald Trump is president. Guess what? For me, Donald Trump has *always* been president.

On January 29, the "airport protest" had taken over Philadelphia International Airport's international terminal in opposition to the Muslim ban. It was one of many occurring that day across the country. Inside, near the baggage claim section, people of color were leading a sit-in. This was different from the protest outside the doors of the terminal, where many people stood obediently behind a police barricade. Inside, the sit-in featured a number of black and brown speakers, each with a personal story of migration or police brutality. One speaker led a chant directed at those behind the police barricade outside: "The Fraternal Order of Police endorsed Donald Trump." Another speaker said, "White liberals are scared of Donald Trump because he's about to make them know what it has always felt like to be black in America."

Time and again, throughout his disastrous term as US president, Trump would take the heat for issues that could not have existed without a two-party consensus. We can see this most clearly on the issue of immigration. In his mission to crack down on "illegal" immigration, Trump promised supporters that he would build a wall along the US-

Mexico border. "And no one builds walls better than me, believe me," he said. Trump supporters believed that education, housing, and healthcare resources should be spent on "true" Americans, not those who came here illegally. Trump's wall-building initiative garnered support among Americans, from workers who more easily blame fellow workers (in this case, migrants) for their difficulties rather than the bosses who profit off cheap migrant labor. These Trump supporters—eager to deport, detain, and criminalize migrants—seemed unconcerned with the hypocrisy of hiring undocumented immigrants as maids and construction workers at Trump's own hotels and golf courses.[10]

The idea that the United States would build a wall at its border to stop illegal immigration struck many civil rights advocates, liberals, and migrants at their core. At anti-Trump demonstrations, signs reading "Walls fall. Always." were waved by protestors. Other signs read, "Build a wall around Trump" or "Show me a 10-foot wall. I'll show you an 11-foot ladder." The outrage against Trump's border wall plan was palpable among US liberals, matched only by the enthusiasm for it among many on the right. We might be horrified by the "build a wall" movement that came to life around Trump. Yet a more historical analysis shows us that this was but the tip of an iceberg that had been building for decades. In fact, anti-immigrant violence runs so deep in the United States that even some among the anti-Trump "resistance" have been participants in it.

Well before Trump's campaign promises, the border wall already existed! Much closer to a fence than a wall, the barricade already stands in many parts along the California-Mexico border. With Trump's promise to build a wall, and the fevered public enthusiasm it inspired, it was as though there "hadn't been a bipartisan government effort over the last quarter-century to put in place an unprecedented array of walls, detection systems, and guards for that southern border."[11] The fear of drug smuggling, the fear of terrorism, the fear of immigrants "taking" American jobs has provided fodder over *decades* to build, secure, and militarize the US-Mexico border. It was under President Bill Clinton that construction of the physical barrier began. Hillary Clinton, as senator, had voted in support of the Secure Fence Act of 2006. Where were the liberal protest signs, signs reading "Walls Must Fall" or "No Walls on Stolen Land," when these *initial* steps toward securing the border were made? Why did it take Trump campaigning on the *explicit* promise to build the wall to spark such widespread opposition?

For the United States, a nation struggling under the weight of mass amnesia, it has seemed far easier to condemn a brash, anti-immigrant figure like Trump than to condemn the entire system of empire-building. It is easier to label Trump's xenophobia "anti-American" than to see it in its greater context. After all, Barack Obama's harsh anti-immigrant policies had earned him the nickname "Deporter-in-Chief," and Joe Biden had supported violent forces in Latin America that forced many to flee to the United States as immigrants.[12] As we saw in chapter 2, mass migration, militarized borders, and gestapo-like immigration forces have been foundational to an American system that existed well before the political career of Donald Trump.

MASS AMNESIA

When George W. Bush announced the US invasion of Iraq in 2003, the anti-war movement sprang to life. As a college student, I found myself swept up in the anti-war demonstrations that erupted in cities around the world. I was stunned to see tens of thousands of people marching down Michigan Avenue in Chicago, blocking traffic, shutting down roads, waving signs of protest, adamant against what they recognized as an illegal, unjustifiable act of violence. By the end of Bush's second term, these anti-war protestors were compelled to do anything to ensure the legacy of Bush wouldn't continue into the next administration. They turned out in huge numbers to support Barack Obama's candidacy. With his campaign of hope and change, many Americans felt Obama would reverse the upsetting fact of American military aggression.

Of course (as we saw in chapter 6), Obama was hardly an anti-war figure. In fact, he expanded the size of the US military and developed new tactics for American warfare. The drone program, for instance, allowed for unmanned planes to carry out bombings in countries like Somalia, Yemen, and Pakistan.[13] Obama endorsed extraordinary rendition and "legalized extra-judicial executions of Muslim terrorist suspects, even if they're American citizens."[14] Especially troubling was the Obama administration's practice of funneling support to rebels in countries whose governments the United States did not support, causing untold instability in these regions (including in Libya and Syria).[15] Such practices were especially troubling as they helped mask US involvement, effectively crushing the chance that the American public might resist it. Where were the thousands in the streets then? Where were the anti-war demonstrations that, under Bush, had brought resisters out from college dorms, suburban homes, and retirement communities? Where were they when American war-making had a more charismatic face? Why does anti-war momentum soften under Democratic administrations, even though *both* parties have expanded American militarism?

In 2008, during a press conference, an Iraqi journalist took off both his shoes and threw them at George W. Bush. The incident became notorious. Liberals and anti-war activists cheered at the act of protest. Around the world, Muntadhar al-Zaidi was hailed a hero. "I didn't know what the guy's cause is," Bush later said, though al-Zaidi had clearly shouted as he launched the second shoe, "This is for the widows and orphans and all those killed in Iraq." (Al-Zaidi was promptly arrested and imprisoned for the act.)

Though it was Bush who stood at the podium that day, perhaps al-Zaidi was throwing his shoes not at Bush alone but at the *entire* apparatus that had so brutally crushed Iraq. He could have just as easily thrown them at Dick Cheney, Bush's vice president, whose company Halliburton made a mint off the Iraq war. He could have thrown them at senators Clinton, Schumer, Biden, and all the Democrats who had voted for the war and the sanctions that came before, plunging Iraq into nutritional and medical crises. He could have thrown them at the *New York Times*, which had published pieces that misled the public into supporting the war on shaky grounds. He could have thrown them at Blackwater, a company whose CEO Erik Prince made a fortune off the Iraq war before becoming a key figure in the Trump administration years later. At the very end of his term, Trump would pardon the convicted Blackwater mercenaries who had opened fire on Iraq civilians, among them a nine-year-old boy whose story is told in the documentary *Blackwater's Youngest Victim*.[16]

From Bush to Obama to Trump, there has been a continued assault on global Muslim populations by the United States. Many feel that it intensified under Obama. As Arun Kundnani puts it, "Neoconservatives invented the terror war, but Obama liberalism normalized it."[17] Yet the upsurge of resistance and anti-war momentum that existed under Bush seemed to vanish during the Obama presidency. Tariq Ali tells us in *The Obama Syndrome* that people held Bush accountable "for policies of unprecedented aggression in the Middle East. In reaction, the election to the presidency of a mixed-race Democrat who vowed to heal America's wounds at home and restore its reputation abroad was greeted with a wave of ideological euphoria not seen since the days of Kennedy." Yet under Obama, "the strategic goals and imperatives of the US imperium remain the same, as do its principal theaters and means of operation."[18] Maha Hilal considers the troubling legacy of Obama's drone warfare program. While Trump expanded the use of drone warfare in Muslim-majority countries, Hilal reminds us that "the abuse of power under one administration leads to abuse of power under another. Trump may be driving it more recklessly, but he's still operating a machine the Obama administration built."[19] Much like Trump, Obama's term saw manyfold increase in the use of drone strikes in comparison to his predecessor.

As Trump's presidency came to an end, liberals assumed a Biden-Harris administration would be less militaristic despite ample evidence to the contrary. Even before his inauguration, Biden had made several cabinet selections who were war hawks, defense contractors, and intelligence officials. Biden made clear in the weeks before being sworn in that his allegiances were to the war industry rather than the anti-war resistance. Much like in 2008, when many Americans placed Islamophobia and "war on terror" crimes squarely in the hands of the Bush administration, in 2020 they would place careless and destructive foreign policy in the hands of Trump. On matters of war and foreign policy, liberal America came to accept Democrats as a "lesser evil." But as reporter Ben Norton put it, "People think of Democrats as the lesser evil, but I think it's more appropriate to think of them as the more effective evil."[20] After all, what could be more effective than being perceived as anti-imperialist while eagerly expanding US empire?

TOWARD A POLITICS OF SUBSTANCE

I won't deny that the *optics* of Trump's presidency were troubling. In chapter 2, we explored the concept of racist dog whistles—coded racist language used by politicians. Under Trump, as journalist Lincoln Blades put it, the dog whistle became a megaphone.[21] Ethnonationalism went from just under the surface to in-your-face, with white nation-alists taking to the streets chanting Nazi slogans. Trump's presidency was punctuated with moments of cringeworthy racism. In 2020, when a Chinese American reporter asked Trump why the United States was lagging behind in COVID-19 testing, he told her to "go ask China," then said that it was a "nasty question."[22] (Throughout the pandemic, Trump had attempted to distract Americans from the US mishandling of the crisis by blaming China for the virus.) Trump called African countries "shitholes," wishing the United States had more immigrants from countries like Norway.[23] It came as little surprise when, in the summer of 2017, Donald Trump's White House would be the first presidential administration in decades not to host a Ramadan dinner.[24] This impetuous form of bigotry made it easy to label Trump a racist.

But in this ease lies a particular danger. Let us go back to the Clin-ton presidency. Bill Clinton, a Democrat, was popularly hailed as a pro-black president. Some even cheekily referred to him as America's "first black president." He spoke of his fondness for jazz, showed off saxo-phone skills, and frequently professed an allegiance with black America. These types of cultural gestures we can call a *politics of form*—that is, they are less about policy commitments and more about superficial acts of pageantry. But what of the *substance* of Bill Clinton's politics? In his first presidential run, Clinton courted Republican support by executing a mentally ill black man, convincing right-wing Americans that he would be "tough on crime."[25] ("Tough on crime" itself is historically an anti-black dog whistle among US politicians.) Years later, when he ran for reelection, Clinton once again sought the Republican vote. He argued that AFDC (the welfare program) be ended so that welfare recipients could exercise "personal responsibility," using many of the same racist dog whistles used by Reagan, implying that poor black mothers were somehow irresponsible and leeching off the state. Clinton slashed welfare programs that had protected countless Americans from recessions and other economic crises. This has only deepened the chasm between America's rich and poor.

An extraordinary focus on political pageantry—Bill Clinton's saxo-phone, Barack Obama's ability to hit a three on the basketball court, George W. Bush's quirky paintings—defines a politics of *form*. But a politics of *substance* would have us look past style and think instead about material issues. Ill-equipped to do this, many Americans would find it much easier to lash out against a singular personality: that of Donald Trump.

It was a politics of form over substance that allowed a self-proclaimed "resistance movement" to emerge among establishment Democrats during the Trump presidency. They labeled themselves a conscious alternative to the dangers of Trump. And during Trump's term, they created some unforgettable spectacles. House Speaker Nancy Pelosi theatrically tore up Donald Trump's State of the Union speech in early 2020. In that moment, Pelosi seemed a bold dissenter, visibly rejecting Trump's political agenda. Yet those familiar with her history were frustrated, as Pelosi had herself voted to deregulate the financial sector, was a staunch opponent of the Medicare for All initiative, and had received gargantuan amounts of financial support from venture capitalists and other corporate donors.[26] In other words, she was neatly aligned with many elements of Trump's agenda. Similarly, CNN's Van Jones openly shed tears of joy when Biden defeated Trump in the election.[27] But just years before, Jones had praised Trump after a speech about the death of a Navy SEAL in Yemen. The United States had been a key player in the war against Yemen, plunging the country into a massive humanitarian crisis. At the time, Van Jones declared that Trump "became president of the United States in that moment, period."[28] Critics of the Yemen war were frustrated by Jones's glorification of Trump. In 2019, Trump's impeachment drew a collection of such resistance figures, people who accused the president of betraying America's core values. Yet many of these figures themselves had been active participants in US empire-building, voting for expanded militarism, or siding with Wall Street over Main Street. To regard them as the resistance asks that we erase "the long US track record of sponsoring foreign military dictatorships, fascist cadres, paramilitary death squads, and other forces generally detrimental to 'democratic values' around the globe," wrote Azeezah Kanji.[29] Said Indian writer Arundhati Roy, "People spend so much time mocking Trump or waiting for him to be impeached. And the danger with that kind of obsession with a single person is that you don't see the system that produced him."[30] Roy's words would be especially prescient for the dynamics that surfaced in the 2020 election.

TRUMP, BIDEN, AND THE 2020 PRESIDENTIAL RACE

In the 2020 presidential race, many Democratic candidates squared off to secure the party's nomination. One of these was Pete Buttigieg, mayor of an Indiana town and the first openly gay presidential candidate. He was interviewed by Mehdi Hasan, whom many regard as a hard-hitting, truth-telling journalist. Hasan asked Buttigieg about Trump's Islamophobia, to which the mayor replied, "Unfortunately it has become far too acceptable to trade in Islamophobia. And cynical politicians have stoked it in order to gain some kind of short-term political advantage, which only plays into the logic of terrorism that is designed to distance us from our own values and undermine pluralism in our country."[31] Based upon this interview alone, Buttigieg seemed unequivocally opposed to anti-Muslim racism. But the "adversarial" journalist did not, in this interview, engage Buttigieg on some of the most devastating elements of his own personal and professional history. Sarah Lazare wrote in *Jacobin* about Mayor Pete's anti-China fearmongering (an increasing obsession for the US foreign policy elite), his support for the devastating and misguided war on terror, and his desire to increase US funding for Israeli colonialism.[32] Yet this interview gave Mayor Pete space to flex his performative politics, blotting out his own record and seducing Muslim voters who accepted his words at face value.

Time and again, pageantry would prevail over practice, form over substance, in the 2020 election cycle. When Joe Biden won the nomination, his choice of running mate made his priorities patently clear. At the time, the nation was rocked with stunning anti-racist protests following the police murder of George Floyd. These uprisings forced the public to ask why America's police budgets are so bloated, while school, housing, and public health initiatives are gutted, and why America has the largest prison population in the world.[33] Amid these reckonings, Biden selected as VP Kamala Harris, whose prior record as a prosecutor was so vicious that it earned her the nickname "Copmala" among many black organizers.[34] Yet the politically savvy Harris was able to fine-tune her public facade, directing the bulk of Americans' attention away from her political record to her quirky choice of sneakers worn on the campaign trail.

Muslim Americans, by and large, came out in support of the Biden-Harris ticket. Following the harrowing Islamophobia of the Trump administration, many of them felt any alternative to Trump would do. Others were genuinely enthusiastic, believing that Biden and Harris offered a serious challenge to anti-Muslim racism. Certainly, when it came to the overtures of their campaign, Biden and Harris seemed committed to reversing the major Islamophobic elements of the Trump administration. One of Biden's first acts after inauguration was to cancel the Muslim ban. Yet at the 2020 Democratic National Convention (DNC), the lineup of speakers was a who's-who of Iraq war crimes. (Colin Powell, for instance, took the stage—in spite of having lied to the United Nations in order to justify the US invasion of Iraq in 2003.)[35] Around the same time, then-senator Harris rejected a moderate cut in military spending to fund social programs for communities impacted by the COVID-19 pandemic. She was also found to have a close relationship to the Center for a New American Security, an organization that has pushed for anti-democratic military action around the world.[36] The DNC also offered a harsh rebuke to the Boycott, Divestment, and Sanctions (BDS) movement, which many Americans—Muslim and non-Muslim—regard as a crucial strategy to challenge Israel's human rights violations against the Palestinian people.[37] And while Donald Trump's presidency saw a cozy alliance with right-wing Narendra Modi's anti-Muslim government in India, Biden and Harris seemed likely to continue this association. In fact, Modi's alliance with the United States has its roots in the Obama presidency.[38]

Yet Biden's selection of Harris as running mate was eagerly celebrated by many Muslim Americans because of her identity as a woman of color. Mehdi Hasan tweeted on the day of Harris's inauguration to the vice presidency, "The daughter of a South Indian immigrant, who eats idlis and dosas, just got sworn in as vice president of the United States." Wajahat Ali, a prominent Muslim American spokesperson, similarly chimed in, "Kamala Harris is a Black and Desi woman. So, let me also enjoy the fact that we're going to have someone who knows her mirch and masala in the White House." Her identity alone was held out as a promise.

At the start of this chapter, we explored the feminist defenses of Hillary Clinton. Let us return now to the question of imperialist feminism. Imperialist feminism celebrates and pushes for the rise of women to high-ranking positions, often in government or corporate leadership. Regardless of what these positions ask them to do, imperialist feminists will celebrate the women who assume them. In 2019, it was reported that the defense industry was headed by women executives. The CEOs of Northrop Grumman, Lockheed Martin, and other weapons and defense contractors were women, a fact celebrated by imperialist feminists. A piece in *Politico* called it "a watershed for what has always been a male-dominated bastion, the culmination of decades of women entering science and engineering fields and knocking down barriers."[39] But for critical feminists, this focus missed the devastating role the arms industry has on the lives of women—especially women in the regions impacted by US militarism. The ascendance of Vice President Kamala Harris reinvigorated these debates, with some claiming that her identity alone was a sign of progress, and others arguing that her brown skin was being used as a grand distraction from her political practices.

These debates require us to think closely about our own political commitments. Do we believe that those in elected office—especially those who have cozy relationships with military contractors, fossil fuel companies, and Wall Street—should be celebrated as icons or leaders of social justice movements? Or do we believe that elected officials will do what is just only when pushed to do so through the concerted efforts of organized, indignant masses? Historian Howard Zinn writes:

> Would I support one candidate against another? Yes, for two minutes—the amount of time it takes to pull the lever down in the voting booth. But before and after those two minutes, our time, our energy, should be spent in educating, agitating, organizing our fellow citizens in the workplace, in the neighborhood, in the schools. Our objective should be to build . . . a movement that, when it reaches a certain critical mass, would shake whoever is in the White House, in Congress, into changing national policy on matters of war and social justice.[40]

In 2020, the Democrats ran a fierce campaign not against Trump but against his personality. Trump pushed for environmentally devastating policy, but Biden, too, ran campaign ads promising he wouldn't ban fracking, a practice that climate scientists have roundly condemned as a danger to our environment. Trump imposed violent anti-immigrant actions at the US-Mexico border, but many of these built upon Obama-era policy. Trump championed his relationship with the brutal regime of Saudi Arabia, but Democrats and Republicans alike have overseen gargantuan arms deals to the regime of a country that wouldn't exist were it not for the ambitions of the US State Department.[41] For conscious Americans, the choice in the 2020 election wasn't much of a choice at all. During this election cycle, professor Cornel West was asked about the troubling record on both sides of the aisle, to which he responded:

> I think we're forced to vote for Biden. But we're not going to *lie* about Biden. We're not going to lie about Harris. We're going to tell the truth about their captivity and about their refusal to hit Pentagon money spending and militarism around the world. Their refusal to hit Wall Street greed and their refusal to speak substantively on issues of poverty.[42]

THE US POLICE STATE

In the weeks following Trump's inauguration in 2017, I noticed more of my students asking questions like, "What is fascism?" and "What is antifa?" (The latter is short for anti-fascist; antifa is a collection of activists who believe *direct* action is needed to prevent the rise of fascism.) With Trump as president and his reckless racial demagoguery, many believed a new fascist order was on the horizon. But for those who had been paying close attention to the gut-wrenching history that has produced America, fascism has always been on the horizon. The internment of Japanese Americans during World War II on the basis of race: was that fascist? What do we make of Andrew Jackson's face on the $20 bill, as he authorized some of the most egregious violence against Native Americans? Does that have elements of fascism? Was it fascist that the United States, a state that now celebrates the legacy of Nelson Mandela as a freedom fighter, had placed him on *a terrorist watchlist* until the year 2008? Was the PATRIOT Act, voted into law and supported by politicians from across the political spectrum, fascist?

We don't have to look far to find that an authoritarian, racist, militaristic America predates Trump. Let us think about what happened in Ferguson in 2014. When the Missouri town broke into an uprising after the murder of teenager Mike Brown by officer Darren Wilson, the police response to the protests was striking. They emerged armed with military-grade assault weapons.[43] They had tear-gas canisters. They wore camouflage. In other words, the police who responded to the Ferguson uprising were strikingly militarized. Across the nation, police have been steadily inching toward greater militarization for decades.[44] The 1980s and 1990s saw a war on drugs that delivered more weaponry and funding for law enforcement. After 9/11, under the guise of anti-terrorism, the military would again increase its supply of surplus weapons to local law enforcement. Local and state law enforcement often found themselves receiving training from the Israeli military, revealing an increasingly close tie between law enforcement and war-making.[45] Americans worried about the rise of an authoritarian state under Trump should have been asking about it well before his campaign began. Before Trump's inauguration, a Justice Department investigation of the Chicago Police Department (CPD) revealed that many on Chicago's South Side saw the police as an "occupying force," and that police presence made their neighborhood feel like an "open-air prison."[46] Even everyday acts like walking to the corner store could lead a black Chicagoan in these neighborhoods to be harassed, handcuffed, or interrogated. Is *this* fascism?

I'm reminded of what took place at the City University of New York (CUNY) in 2011. Students had planned to attend a Board of Trustees meeting in order to speak against a sharp tuition hike that the board was attempting to pass. The original mission of the university was to provide free or low-cost higher education to New York City residents. When I, along with other students, professors, and community members, arrived to attend the meeting, the building was lined with security guards holding batons and security officials in suits speaking into walkie-talkies. They told us we wouldn't be allowed to attend the meeting, which is (by policy) open to the campus community. A young college student spoke to those of us who had gathered. "If they won't let us into that meeting that we are allowed to attend, let's all sit down in this lobby and have the meeting right here." The act of civil disobedience didn't last long. As soon as we had taken our seats in the lobby, the slew of security guards and, seemingly out of nowhere, NYPD cops in riot gear, stomped through the meeting, arresting many of us. One officer stepped on my hand, sending searing pain through my arm. Within minutes I found myself pinned against the wall, a cop's baton across my chest. "Get the fuck out!" he screamed at me. "You have me pinned against a wall," I responded, recording the interaction. Think about it: these cops and private security guards showed up en masse to crush a small gathering of college students who wanted to protest a *tuition hike*, not overthrow the government. Was *this* fascism?

As we have seen in this chapter, identifying the continuities in our racial past is as important as identifying the ruptures. We might, for instance, be better prepared to reform our immigration system if we saw the overlaps between Democratic and Republican administrations—both in how they treat immigrants who arrive at our borders and their policies vis-à-vis those countries from which migrants flee. Looking at the history of anti-black racism, we might do the same: the way the US system of slavery was "ended" only to morph into the Black Codes, sundown towns,[47] and today's "new Jim Crow" system of mass incarceration.[48] When it comes to Islamophobia, the accusations of anti-Muslim racism hurled at Trump make no sense unless we also consider the vast expansions of US state power that were authorized by both Bush and Obama. As Alex Emmons wrote in the *Intercept*, "Commander-in-Chief Donald Trump Will Have Terrifying Powers. Thanks, Obama."[49] An unprecedented surveillance apparatus, the legalization of torture (under pretty nicknames like "enhanced interrogation"), or the expansion of anti-immigrant legislation were all in plain sight before the Trump presidency, with little in the way of public outcry.

We thus see how Trump—with his buffoonish outbursts and in-your-face racism—was able to distract Americans from the fact that, in many ways, he was upholding a long history of xenophobia, anti-black racism, and expansion of US militarism. This has been a foundational element of both political parties and the administrations that came before him. This is a painful reckoning, for it means that dismantling the systems of injustice will not be as easy as voting in an election or the impeachment of an individual. To quote a common chant at anti-war and anti–police brutality protests, "The whole damn system is guilty as hell."

8

THE NEVER-ENDING WAR ON TERROR

Public school students near Washington, DC, study the arc of a missile as part of their math lesson on parabolas. In another classroom, students consider a hypothetical terrorist attack on a US airport.[1] Professor Nicole Nguyen writes about the transformation of schools across the country in the years since 9/11. She finds that American schools have partnerships with the defense industry (companies like Lockheed Martin and Northrop Grumman) to support their science and math classes. The classes thus inevitably produce students who feel under threat of a potential terrorist attack or compelled to support US foreign policy. They are offered, in Nguyen's words, a "curriculum of fear." And for those who continue on to college, the university setting isn't all that different. Henry Giroux writes that universities since 9/11 have been increasingly shaped by compulsory patriotism and militarization.[2] Otherwise cash-strapped universities receive mountains of funding for research centers that develop weapons or technology for the defense industry, for instance. Like the public schools Nguyen studies, Giroux exposes the close overlaps between Pentagon funding, US intelligence agencies, and colleges and universities across the country. The war on terror seems to be just about everywhere, even in American classrooms.

But what *is* the "war on terror"? Yes, the term includes official wars (like those waged in Afghanistan and Iraq) and other, murkier military initiatives (like drone warfare or US funding to rebel groups to fight the foreign enemies of the United States). But beyond these, our definition of the war on terror must include the entire array of responses—within the United States and around the world—that have been waged in the name of fighting terrorism since 9/11. When defined this way, the war on terror's battlefields seem endless. They include the expanding prisons and police budgets in the United States, often under the guise of counterterrorism. They also include the increased scrutiny of immigrants under the justification of homeland security. And while the war on terror has been ostensibly waged as a response to the terrorist attacks of 9/11/2001, as we will see, it has outlived this justification. The war on terror has even outlived its name. George W. Bush first used the term just five days after the September 11 attacks. By his second term, Obama declared the war on terror (officially called "Operation Enduring Freedom") done, though in practice, he kept intact its major components, even expanding many of them. Under a series of different titles, the war on terror continued through the Trump presidency and into the Biden administration. Note that both Democratic and Republican administrations have been at its helm.

This chapter offers a quick guide to understanding the perpetual war on terror, especially for generations too young to remember a time before it existed. We trace here the porous boundaries of what "fighting terrorism" has meant: on battlefields, in schools, and in the hearts and minds of those asked to support it. My hope is that reflecting on the first two decades of the terror wars will allow us look at them from a distance, to examine the crucial role they've played in shaping our current realities.

TWO DECADES OF THE PERMANENT WAR

Comedian George Carlin joked about Americans, "We like war. We are a war-like people. We like war because we're good at it. And you know why we're good at it? Because we have a lot of practice!"[3] Beginning with wars against the indigenous inhabitants, US history is a series of military initiatives, each leading to a permanent expansion in the size and scale of the military itself. At the time of this writing, as the country struggled with a pandemic and the crisis of joblessness and poverty it brought, newly inaugurated President Biden promised to keep the Space Force branch of the US military (created by Donald Trump) intact.[4] The Space Force—the US military's outer space division—

would cost close to $16 billion in 2021 alone.[5] Without fail, American schools, hospitals, and public infrastructure are defunded, yet the defense budget soars.

US *militarism* is a wide-ranging set of practices, beliefs, and systems that expand American war-making. Militarism describes the entire apparatus of warfare—going well beyond "official" military components like weaponry, soldiers, and army bases. At NFL games, the air force will often do a showy flyover displaying their latest bomber aircraft while members of the armed forces stand in a military salute as the "Star-Spangled Banner" is played.[6] The Department of Defense works closely with Hollywood directors, providing them equipment and funding while reviewing their scripts, ultimately shaping the image and perception of American warfare for moviegoers. While military-themed films are among those vetted by the Department of Defense, so too are episodes of *Jeopardy* or *The Price Is Right*.[7] The military analysts who appear on mainstream news programs often have close relationships with the Pentagon, or are themselves ex-military officials.[8] In his book *The United States of War*, David Vine reminds us that the American towns with "Fort" in their name often mark a site of battle between European settlers and the original indigenous inhabitants.[9] What used to be called the Department of War was renamed the Department of Defense in 1949; thus, many see it as a *protective* force rather than an *offensive* one. So militaristic is the United States that when the COVID-19 pandemic brought disastrous unemployment and poverty, a 10 percent decrease in the US military budget to address this recession was roundly rejected by a bipartisan majority in Congress.[10] For just a few weeks of US military spending, the country could have paid the medical bills of any American with COVID-19. It is against this backdrop of militarism that we ought to understand the war on terror.

Afghanistan, invaded shortly after 9/11, was its first major battleground. However, this country was no stranger to war. The British, at the height of their empire, had sought control of the region, waging battles often fought by Indian soldiers who were themselves subjects of British colonial rule.[11] Over a century later, the United States would begin its many incursions into Afghanistan. President Jimmy Carter's administration wanted the Soviet Union (also known as the USSR, then the major rival of the United States) to suffer "its own Vietnam." In other words, the United States wished to see the USSR lose money, lives, and morale fighting an unwinnable war—just as the United States had done in Vietnam.[12] As mentioned in chapter 6, the United States began funding religious extremists known as the mujahideen in the 1980s, arming and training them to fight the Soviets. The United States even provided schoolbooks, one entitled "The Alphabet for Jihad Literacy," to children in the region. These books included reading lessons like "my uncle does jihad with his gun," indoctrinating in these youth a holy war mentality against the USSR.[13] This was a "proxy war," one the United States fought indirectly by funding and training the fighters. During this proxy war, Osama bin Laden found a close alliance with the United States, such that he and the mujahideen were deemed freedom fighters.[14] Bin Laden later formed Al-Qaeda, the organization behind the 9/11 attacks, which prompted the 2001 US invasion of Afghanistan. The war in Afghanistan would become the longest in US history. In 2019, secret documents revealed that the government had been lying to the American public about the Afghan war effort, making false claims of victories and hiding evidence of losses.[15]

The 2003 invasion of Iraq came next, despite Iraq having no connection to acts of terrorism against the United States. At this time, many Americans came to see Iraqi leader Saddam Hussein as a bogeyman, a barbaric dictator to be removed from power at all costs. Those who didn't agree with the US campaign against Iraq were labeled traitors. When France refused to join in invading Iraq, Americans renamed French fries "freedom fries."[16] A historical analysis, once again, took a backseat to patriotism. In fact, the United States had handpicked Saddam Hussein to oppose a man named Abd al-Karim Qasim in the early 1960s. Qasim's dreams of an Iraq that controlled its own oil reserves threatened unfettered US access to the country's natural resources. The United States wanted him out, and recruited Hussein to oppose him. With Qasim out of the picture, Saddam Hussein enjoyed decades of US support, even as he committed some of the most genocidal elements of his rule.[17] As mentioned in chapter 6, the United States only stopped providing support in 1991 when Hussein went against US interests in Kuwait, resulting in years of sanctions and devastation for the Iraqi people. This history would make things awkward for the US political establishment. George W. Bush's Defense Secretary Donald Rumsfeld was flabbergasted when, in 2002, an old video surfaced of him warmly shaking hands with a smiling Saddam Hussein. At this time, in 2003,

Rumsfeld was busy convincing the American public that Hussein was an imminent, unparalleled threat. "Where did you get this video?" he asks the CNN correspondent uncomfortably, then adds, "Isn't that interesting? . . . There I am."[18] The war in Iraq would be so disastrous that even its chief architects (Joe Biden, for instance) would be forced to express remorse for it.[19]

While Iraq and Afghanistan loom large as battlegrounds of the war on terror, its terrain has stretched well past these two sites. The Philippines, Pakistan, Yemen, Somalia, Sudan, and countless other nations have been part of Operation Enduring Freedom. We must also remember that the impact of the terror wars extends beyond the direct costs of combat. Indirect costs must also figure into our assessment of the war on terror. Writes Andrea Mazzarino of the Cost of War Project:

> People die in childbirth because hospitals or clinics have been destroyed. They die because there are no longer the doctors or the necessary equipment to detect cancer early enough or even more common problems like infections. They die because roads have been bombed or are unsafe to travel on. They die from malnutrition because farms, factories, and the infrastructure to transport food have all been reduced to rubble. They die because the only things available and affordable to anesthetize them from emotional and physical pain may be opioids, alcohol, or other dangerous substances. They die because the healthcare workers who might have treated them for, or immunized them against, once obsolete illnesses like polio have been intimidated from doing their work. And of course, as is evident from our own skyrocketing military suicide rates, they die by their own hands.[20]

One of the most perverse manifestations of the terror wars was the creation of a prison at the US Naval Base at Guantanamo Bay, Cuba. It was built by an oil company called Halliburton that (in the early "war on terror" days) was also contracted to construct prisons and internment camps around the world. Many found it troubling that Bush's vice president, Dick Cheney, had once been Halliburton's CEO.[21] At the Guantanamo Bay Detention Center, detainees were imprisoned for years even after being found innocent and cleared for release. So gruesome were the tactics used at the prison (including, for instance, blasting music for hours on end at maximum volume, sleep deprivation, and force feeding) that it could only exist "over there," far away from US laws on treatment of prisoners.[22] The torture tactics used at the prison have been carefully documented in *Guantanamo Diary*, a memoir by Mohamedou Ould Slahi, who was held at Guantanamo without charge for fourteen years.

I couldn't do the war on terror justice in a single book chapter, and certainly not in this introductory volume on Islamophobia. (The reader will find far more in-depth sources in this chapter's citations.) Instead, the outline above is meant to provide context as we turn to the next section. We will consider here how life in the United States has been shaped by the war on terror, especially as it has impacted national memory. What has it meant to come of age amid this never-ending war? How do Americans understand, and perhaps more crucially, misunderstand the US response to 9/11?

NEVER FORGET

It's commonplace for Americans to recall where they were and what they were doing at the time of the 9/11 attacks. There also exists an entire industry of memorializing 9/11. Rest stop shops along the New Jersey Turnpike still carry "Never Forget"–themed memorabilia. The 9/11 Memorial & Museum store sells 9/11-themed pins, sweatshirts, flags, and T-shirts.[23] In 2020, the store updated its merchandise to include face masks during the COVID-19 outbreak, which at its peak was killing as many Americans per day as died on 9/11. The masks were printed with such phrases as "in darkness we shine brightest—9/11 memorial" and "NYC Strong." Globally, at least twelve hundred memorials are dedicated to 9/11, including at sites in Israel, Canada, and the US embassy in Kabul.[24] Of the two hundred thousand tons of steel that lay in the wreckage of the Twin Towers, much was parceled out and sent to memorial sites around the world.[25] Many churches, museums, public schools, and US military bases have 9/11 memorials that showcase these pieces of steel from the World Trade Center.

Yet one could visit these memorials and still learn nothing about the roots of the 9/11 attacks: the US-Afghan relations that gave rise to the mujahideen;[26] the decades-long relationship between the United States and Saudi Arabia;[27] the righteous indignation across the Middle East about Israeli settler colonialism.[28] These have been sliced out of the appropriate, permissible memory of 9/11. It's as though, writes Catherine Lutz, "the people who jumped from those downtown workplace windows flew free of history" (724).[29]

On the morning of the attacks, *The Howard Stern Show* was on air. When the second plane struck, Stern and his stylist went on a tirade about kicking the "towel head bastards" out of this country:

> We're totally too lax in this country. This is war. It's the Japanese. This is Pearl Harbor. Now is not the time to even ask questions. Drop a few atomic bombs. Do a few chemical warfare hits. Let their people suffer until they understand. Blow them all to sky high! Atom bombs! Just do it so they're flattened and turned into a paved road. And we can take the oil for ourselves.[30]

As we see here, racism, militarism, and plunder instantly became knee-jerk responses to 9/11.

Americans are asked to treat the memory of 9/11 as sacred. When Somali American US representative Ilhan Omar discussed the Islamophobia that followed 9/11, she came under attack for using the phrase "some people did something" to describe the events. Her critics included a man who lost his mother in the 9/11 attacks. He wore a shirt that read "some people did something" at a Ground Zero memorial ceremony as he made clear that "our constitutional freedoms were attacked and our nation's founding on Judeo-Christian principles was attacked. That's what some people did. Got that now?"[31] The *New York Post* ran a headline with Omar's quote, followed by "Here's your something: 2,977 people dead by terrorism." The story was accompanied by a cover picture of the World Trade Center burning after the attacks.[32] Omar, a black Muslim woman, had broken the rules about the *appropriate* way to remember 9/11.

As the twentieth anniversary of 9/11 approached, I became increasingly curious about how generations who came of age after the attacks understood the legacy of 9/11 and the war on terror. I was especially interested in what they'd learned about it in their classroom. Soon after 9/11, dozens of state legislatures introduced bills to push school lessons to be more patriotically themed.[33] Weeks after 9/11, a House resolution passed urging schools across the country to display "God Bless America" banners.[34] Meanwhile, teachers were suspended for opposing the

2003 invasion of Iraq.[35] A high school student was suspended for wearing a T-shirt that read, "WITH LIBERTY AND JUSTICE FOR
SOME, NOT ALL."[36] This climate was especially draconian for Muslim, Arab, and South Asian students. A Palestinian student faced harsh
discipline after he was misheard saying "terrorist" instead of "tourist,"
and Palestinian students who made drawings of the 9/11 attacks—
something many young students were doing in their art classes—were
disciplined for their art.[37]

Many Americans complete a K–12 education without ever having a
lesson about 9/11 or the ensuing war on terror. Textbooks often provide
more information about Pearl Harbor than about 9/11.[38] When such
lessons do exist, they are typically oriented toward fear, grief, or a celebration of American values.[39] Students commemorate the lives lost on
9/11, decorate red-white-and-blue cupcakes, or make American flags as
art projects. In 2019, New York governor Andrew Cuomo signed a law
mandating public schools to have a moment of silence every 11th of
September.[40] "By establishing this annual day of remembrance and a
brief moment of silence in public schools, we will help ensure we never
forget—not just the pain of that moment but of the courage, sacrifice
and outpouring of love that defined our response," he said. One middle
school assignment on the tenth anniversary of the attacks asked students to write an essay evaluating the construction of a mosque near
Ground Zero.[41] Curricula for K–12 teachers made by the Department
of Education in 2011 encouraged them to connect September 11 and
Constitution Day (September 17) and to use the lessons to teach that
"in contrast to people in many other nations, to be an American does
not mean one is a member of a particular racial, religious, or ethnic
group."[42] Meanwhile, in a comprehensive study of school textbooks,
"none of the texts . . . challenged students to critically examine the roots
of the attacks or to analyze the external policies of the United States."[43]

My study of 103 college students (born between 1998 and 2002)
further reveals what they know about 9/11 and the war on terror. They
responded to open-ended questions about Osama bin Laden, the
events of 9/11, the USA PATRIOT Act, the 2003 invasion of Iraq, and
the 2001 invasion of Afghanistan. Many of them admitted to being
unclear on several items with such statements as, "I honestly don't know
why we invaded Iraq," or "To be honest, I was never taught about the
war on terror." Some assumed that ISIS was behind 9/11, though ISIS

itself emerged in Iraq *following* the 2003 US invasion. Notably, nearly a fifth believed Iraq or Saddam Hussein was responsible for the 9/11 attacks. Some suggested Iraq was invaded in 2003 because of Saddam Hussein's acts of aggression against the United States ("the US wanted to get Saddam out because of his terroristic acts against America"). This reflects the persistent attempts by the Bush administration to frame Saddam Hussein leading up to the 2003 invasion.[44] The United States has kept alive these Iraq–9/11 linkages, even naming a prison in Iraq after a fire marshal who died in the 9/11 rescue mission and naming a bomb dropped on Iraq after an American 9/11 victim upon the request of the man's father.[45] Iraq has still not been exonerated for 9/11 in America's collective memory.

THE COSTS OF FORGETTING

Notably, not all responses to my study were this vague or unclear. Many respondents were able to regurgitate the precise figure, 2,977, who died in the 9/11 attacks. Nearly 10 percent knew that first responders and survivors of the attacks suffered chronic and painful respiratory illnesses. "I know that firefighters and first responders inhaled dust and fumes that day and they have never been compensated for their troubles," said a respondent who was unable to list a reason for the US invasion of Afghanistan in 2001 or explain what the USA PATRIOT Act was. In remembering the 2,977 dead Americans, the 37 million displaced by the US-led war on terror are erased, as are those victimized at the Abu Ghraib prison, the Guantanamo Bay Detention Center, or through the National Security Entry-Exit Registry System (NSEERS), which rounded up Muslim immigrants across the country following 9/11.

It's telling to see the vividness with which young Americans remember the suffering and loss of the 9/11 attacks alongside their vague knowledge of the conditions that came before or those that followed. Despite the refrain of "Never Forget," it seems Americans have been asked to forget the political realities of the war on terror. In years of teaching about Islamophobia and the war on terror, I've seen countless students perplexed. How is it possible, they ask, that they have grown up *surrounded* by the realities of the war on terror, yet are simultaneously unaware of it? This is one of the key contradictions at the heart of US militarism. Americans are asked to be firm and unwavering in their loyalty to the nation's military practices. Yet they are also asked to remain hazy on the facts that contextualize them. As Howard Stern said while the 9/11 attacks unfolded, "Now is not the time to even ask questions." He echoed the words of George H. W. Bush, who said, "I'll never apologize for the United States of America. Ever. I don't care what the facts are."[46] But, as we will see in our conclusion, it is *always* the time to ask questions, and living at the heart of the US empire, we *must* consistently and unapologetically care what the facts are.

9

CONCLUSION

Inverting Reality, Selling Empire

In 2009, during the height of the conservative Tea Party protests, Glenn Beck, the conservative radio commentator, began a movement called the "9/12 Project."[1] It aimed to return to what Beck called the "spirit of 9/12," referring to the immediate aftermath of September 11, 2001. According to Beck, this was a time when Americans united behind a love for the nation and its founding values. While running for president in 2016, Hillary Clinton would also invoke the spirit of 9/12, asking Americans to return to that moment of togetherness.[2] (It struck many on the Left as peculiar that Clinton would invoke a movement started by an ultraright-wing spokesperson.) Beck and Clinton are correct: there *was* a sort of national unity that unfolded after 9/11. George W. Bush, who had been appointed to the presidency by the Supreme Court rather than elected, saw his approval ratings soar after 9/11, reaching the highest levels seen by any US president in over half a century.[3] Bush demanded this unity, telling Americans shortly after the attacks, "You're either with us or with the terrorists." Many were quick to accept his call. When asked by (then) CNN cohost Tucker Carlson about her position on the Iraq war, Britney Spears summed up the nature of post-9/11 American unity, saying, "Honestly, I think we should just trust our president in every decision he makes."[4]

This book has taken a "view from below" of the spirit of 9/12, exposing the costs of this national unity. The aftermath of 9/11 saw America enter a state of exception, a time when ordinary laws and civil liberties were suspended and a new "security state" was ushered into existence. This included: increased powers of the government to surveil people without cause; the militarization of the border; the crackdown on migrants (often fleeing conditions created by US intervention); and the US president's expanded powers to declare war. Stephen Sheehi reminds us that 9/11 made possible the "justification for stripping the civil liberty of tens of thousands; profiling and illegal detaining of thousands of legal residents; condoning and practicing the torture and kidnapping of suspects; legalizing the spying, surveillance, and entrapment of American citizens; and setting the precedence for the assassination of American citizens."[5] Corey Robin tells us that "what has been most effective in silencing dissent is not so much particular acts of repression by the state or civil society . . . but the *fear* those acts arouse. . . . Fear does the work—or enhances the work—of repression."[6] (He recalls the story of a UCLA employee who was suspended for a week without pay for sending out an email condemning the United States' support for Israel and bombing of Iraq.) During the aftermath of 9/11, anti-Muslim hate crimes increased by 1,600 percent, a level that would be reached again in the immediate aftermath of the Trump inauguration.[7] I urge the reader to peruse the many books that vividly expose the post-9/11 climate: *How Does It Feel to Be a Problem?*, *The Terror Factory*, *Islamophobia: An Ideological Campaign against Muslims*, and *Guantanamo Diary*. In these, the authors have preserved the grotesqueness of the spirit of 9/12, painting a picture of an era with which many Americans are entirely unfamiliar.

In my own life, the spirit of 9/12 meant inevitable "random searches" at airports—being pulled aside for secondary screening, or even having security agents run their fingers through my hair. Without fail, when I deliver a public lecture or am interviewed by the media, I receive hate mail. I'm told to "go back to my country" or accused of being ungrateful for the freedoms given by America.

Nevertheless, in 2020 *New York Times* columnist and renowned economist Paul Krugman tweeted, "Overall, Americans took 9/11 pretty calmly. Notably, there wasn't a mass outbreak of anti-Muslim sentiment and violence, which could have all too easily happened."[8] To anyone who had been paying attention, Krugman's tweet was a perfect inversion of what had *actually* happened.

This chapter reflects upon the upside-down logics, the inversions, that are endemic to America's terror decades. We saw in chapter 8 how the war on terror, ostensibly waged to end terrorism, has in fact *expanded* it. For instance, in the years since 9/11, the United States has even offered support to the very groups it was simultaneously spending trillions to defeat.[9] Waged in the name of "protecting freedoms," the war on terror has in fact rolled them back—both here in the United States, where civil liberties have been curtailed, and around the world, where the United States has expanded its support to dictatorial and anti-democratic forces. Even the very branding of 9/11 as an event we must "never forget" was quite the opposite: forgetting *was* the very point.

At one of my first-ever anti-war protests, in Chicago in 2003, an angry passerby yanked on my sign and hissed at me, "You know, people are fighting that war so that *you* have the right to protest here." But by now we have seen how misguided this statement is—that the United States (with Democrat and Republican leaders alike) has both crushed popular movements in Iraq that threatened American access to the region and silenced anti-war voices at home. Robert Jensen questions the assumption that "they're fighting for our freedoms," asking, "Is the conflict in which the troops are fighting actually being fought to defend the freedom of Americans? And, if it were the case that the freedoms of Americans were at risk, is a war the best way to defend them?"[10] Again, another inversion, as Americans are asked to believe that our military incursions are a *defense* of freedom.

President Bush, addressing the nation after 9/11, said, "America was targeted for attack because we're the brightest beacon for freedom and opportunity in the world." Yet Al-Qaeda had proclaimed the attacks were waged in response to US militarism in Somalia, US military presence in Saudi Arabia, and the expansive American support for Israel.[11] For many Americans, accepting that it was an attack on America's freedoms was far easier to stomach than reflecting on the long history of imperialist violence that compelled a response as ugly as 9/11. The spirit of 9/12 meant sidestepping this discussion entirely; to dissent, to critique, or to offer nuance after 9/11 was to be a traitor. Dissenting professors of Muslim or Arab backgrounds received death threats, were branded anti-American, or faced firing and tenure difficulties—for instance, professors Nadia Abu el Hajj, Joseph Massad, and Sami al-

Arian.[12] To the thinking mind, "they hate our freedoms" was a grand inversion.

We have seen how even the mainstream efforts to fight Islamophobia are upside-down. They often focus on Muslim patriotism, Muslim support for the armed forces, or Muslim American buying power, wealth, and success in the capitalist system. They assume that if non-Muslims understand Muslims better, Islamophobia will crumble. These approaches often take the place of earnest conversations about the politics of empire. The "good Muslim" trope is a reversal of what a serious fight against anti-Muslim racism demands.

Indeed, the entire panic about terrorism sparked after 9/11, and all the resources mobilized to fight it, have been contrary to what a more *appropriate* fear would demand. A true war on terror, an intellectually honest fight against the threats to our safety and survival, would be directed at climate catastrophes. (At the time of this writing, Texas had recently been engulfed by a bitter snowstorm, resulting in mass blackouts for days and made worse by a privatized energy grid that collapsed during the blizzard.)[13] A true war on terror would fight the wealth gap between rich and poor, a chasm that grew even further during the coronavirus pandemic, as those at the very top saw their shares of wealth explode while food insecurity, unemployment, and housing crises threatened the well-being of a record number of ordinary Americans.[14] Americans are taught to believe that China, Russia, or Iran constitute threats to our well-being. But, says Iraq War veteran Mike Prysner:

> The real enemy is here. Poor and working people in this country are sent to kill poor and working people in another country, to make the rich richer. The enemy is the system that sends us to war when it's profitable. They're the insurance companies that deny us healthcare when it's profitable. They're the banks that take our homes when it's profitable.[15]

Perhaps the war on terror was fought to distract us from these existential threats.

One of the greatest skills critical thinking provides, says Steven Salaita, "is the ability to recognize bullshit."[16] We have called bullshit on many things in this book: the cynical attempts to use "patriotic" Muslims to gloss over state violence; the focus on "culture talk" rather than material realities of the war on terror; and the erasure of the roots of the terror motivating the attacks of 9/11/2001. As Moustafa Bayoumi says, the global war on terror has been "designed to make us stupid."[17] The unthinking mind made it possible to round up Muslim immigrants for indefinite detention, swell the military budget, and spread apathy about the devastating drone warfare program. The terror wars could not have been waged had the public been ready to think about the history of US involvement in Afghanistan, the relationship between Saudi Arabia and the United States, or the expansion of US military bases around the world. "The United States," Robert Jensen tells us,

> is a society in which people not only can get by without knowing much about the wider world but are systematically encouraged not to think independently or critically and instead to accept the mythology of the United States as a benevolent, misunderstood giant as it lumbers around the world trying to do good. That means the crisis in which we find ourselves after 9/11 is not only political but intellectual, a problem not just of doing but of knowing.[18]

When the next crisis strikes—say, a terror attack targeting Americans—what will those of us who live at the heart of empire do? Will we support legislation to expand racial profiling? Will we fork over our tax dollars to a bloated war machine? Or will we remember the grand failure of each of these strategies and instead arm ourselves with a critical consciousness?

Imagine if we allowed ourselves to ask, even in times of crisis, the questions we are told are too impractical to ask: What if prisons and policing weren't solutions to the things we call "crime"? How would the world look if the US military budget didn't tower over those of the several largest world militaries *combined*? What are ways to prevent terrorism that don't involve surveillance, racial profiling, detention, or torture? What if wealth weren't concentrated in increasingly fewer hands, while more and more Americans' lives crumble under the weight of medical and education debt?

In 2021, the Justice for Muslims Collective worked with several organizations to issue an agenda entitled "Abolishing the War on Terror & Building Communities of Care."[19] It called for a halt to new prison construction; an end to pretrial detention; support for indigenous groups who have seen land treaties violated by the US government; a robust COVID relief bill to ensure safe working conditions and unemployment assistance; and the closing of the detention center at Guantanamo Bay. Such demands do not focus on themes of tolerance, privilege, or placing brown and black faces in seats of power in the United States, which, as we have seen, only enable the inversions demanded by the imperialist state. Instead, this platform draws attention to the interconnections of American racism: how anti-black, anti-Muslim, and anti-immigrant racism are issues of economic and legal justice.

This is a promising turn in the work of anti-Islamophobia organizing in the United States. It is what Sohail Daulatzai and Junaid Rana speak of in their call to create a "Muslim Left"[20]: a tradition that draws from the legacies of Malcolm X, Faiz Ahmed Faiz, Suheir Hammad, Yassin Bey, and Rasmea Odeh—all figures who resisted the injustices of empire, capitalism, and racism. In this tradition, that of the Muslim Left, we find a well-worn path, one that empowers us to call bullshit on the inverted realities that have been spun in the terror decades since 9/11.

NOTES

PREFACE

1. Stephen Sheehi, *Islamophobia: The Ideological Campaign against Muslims* (Atlanta: Clarity Press, 2011).

2. Equal Justice Initiative, *Lynching in America: Confronting the Legacy of Racial Terror* (Montgomery, AL: Equal Justice Initiative, 2015).

3. Ian Haney López, *Dog Whistle Politics: How Coded Racial Appeals Have Reinvented Racism and Wrecked the Middle Class* (Oxford: Oxford University Press, 2015).

4. Peter Getzels and Eduardo López, dirs., *Harvest of Empire: A History of Latinos in America* (Onyx Films, EVS Communications, and Loquito Productions, 2012); Juan González, *Harvest of Empire: A History of Latinos in America* (New York: Penguin, 2000).

I. INTRODUCTION

1. David Graham, "The Empathy Gap between Paris and Beirut," *Atlantic*, November 16, 2015.

2. I hesitate to use the phrase *9/11* as shorthand for the events in New York City, in Pennsylvania, and at the Pentagon on September 11, 2001, which problematically erases the historical and political relevance of other events that took place on that date in other times and places. I do this for the sake of readability.

3. Gilbert Achcar, *The Clash of Barbarisms: The Making of the New World Disorder* (New York: Routledge, 2015).

4. Tessa Berenson, "Trump: US May Have to Do 'Unthinkable' in Light of Paris Attack," *Time*, November 19, 2015, http://time.com/4120711/donald-trump-paris-attack-muslims.

5. Ed O'Keefe, "Ben Carson: U.S. Should Block Middle Eastern Refugees after Paris Attacks," *Washington Post*, November 13, 2015, https://www.washingtonpost.com/news/post-politics/wp/2015/11/13/ben-carson-u-s-should-block-middle-eastern-refugees-after-paris-attacks.

6. Edward Said, *Orientalism* (New York: Vintage, 1978).

7. Pem Buck, *In/Equality: An Alternative Anthropology* (Palo Cedro, CA: CAT Publishing, 2013).

8. Jeanne Theoharis, *The Rebellious Life of Mrs. Rosa Parks* (Boston: Beacon Press, 2013).

9. The MOVE Organization is a Philadelphia group that believes in communalism, antiracism, animal rights, and several other liberation-based philosophies.

10. The documentary film *Let the Fire Burn* provides a rich historical account of the MOVE bombing and the gross violations of human rights on the part of Philadelphia city officials. *Let the Fire Burn*, directed by Jason Osder (New York: Zeitgeist Films, 2013).

11. At the time of this writing, the City of Philadelphia had yet to follow through on a year-old promise to move the statue away from City Hall to a new location.

12. Equal Justice Initiative, *Lynching in America: Confronting the Legacy of Racial Terror* (Montgomery, AL: Equal Justice Initiative, 2015).

13. Tariq Ali, *The Clash of Fundamentalisms: Crusades, Jihads, and Modernity* (London: Verso, 2002).

14. Jack Shaheen, *Guilty: Hollywood's Verdict on Arabs after 9/11* (Northampton, MA: Interlink Publishing, 2012).

15. *Inside Man*, directed by Spike Lee (Hollywood, CA: Universal Studios, 2006).

16. Arun Kundnani, *The Muslims Are Coming! Islamophobia, Extremism, and the Domestic War on Terror* (New York: Verso, 2014), 252.

17. Steven Salaita, *Anti-Arab Racism in the USA: Where It Comes from and What It Means for Politics Today* (London: Pluto, 2006), 10–11.

18. Arsalan Iftikhar, "America's 'Dirty Arab' Islamophobia Problem," *Islamic Monthly*, August 17, 2016, http://www.theislamicmonthly.com/americas-dirty-arab-islamophobia-problem.

19. Salaita, *Anti-Arab Racism*, 10–11.

20. Hamid Dabashi, *Brown Skin, White Masks* (London: Pluto), 2011.

21. *Meet the Press*, NBC, October 19, 2008; Maureen Dowd, "Moved by a Crescent," *New York Times*, October 21, 2008.

22. Ben Smith, "Muslims Barred from Picture at Obama Event," *Politico*, June 18, 2008, http://www.politico.com/story/2008/06/muslims-barred-from-picture-at-obama-event-011168.

23. Junaid Rana, *Terrifying Muslims: Race and Labor in the South Asian Diaspora* (Durham, NC: Duke University Press, 2011).

24. Michael A. Gomez, "Muslims in Early America," *Journal of Southern History* 60, no. 4 (1994): 671–710.

25. Richard B. Turner, "Edward Wilmot Blyden and Panafricanism: The Ideological Roots of Islam and Black Nationalism in the United States," *Muslim World* 87, no. 2 (1997): 169–82.

26. Sulayman S. Nyang, *Islam in the United States of America* (Chicago: Kazi Publications, 1999).

27. Audrey Singer and Jill H. Wilson, "From 'There' to 'Here': Refugee Resettlement in Metropolitan America" (Washington, DC: Brookings Institution, 2006).

28. Patrick Bowen, "US Latino/a Muslims since 1920: From 'Moors' to 'Latino Muslims,'" *Journal of Religious History* 37, no. 2 (2013): 165–84.

29. Ali, *Clash of Fundamentalisms*, 300.

2. THE VISUAL POLITICS OF RACISM AND ISLAMOPHOBIA

1. Fred Barbash, "Muslim Ban Language Suddenly Disappears from Campaign Website," *Washington Post*, May 9, 2017, https://www.washingtonpost.com/news/morning-mix/wp/2017/05/09/trumps-preventing-muslim-immigration-vow-disappears-from-campaign-website-after-spicer-questioned/?utm_term=.32d190ccf616.

2. Natasha Hall, "Refugees Are Already Vigorously Vetted. I Know Because I Vetted Them," *Washington Post*, February 1, 2017, https://www.washingtonpost.com/posteverything/wp/2017/02/01/refugees-are-already-vigorously-vetted-i-know-because-i-vetted-them/?utm_term=.aa147dfc5122.

3. Zaid Jilani, "Former Racial-Profiling Critic Geraldo Rivera Now Supports Profiling Muslims," *Think Progress*, January 8, 2010, https://thinkprogress.org/former-racial-profiling-critic-geraldo-rivera-now-supports-profiling-muslims-thats-just-the-way-it-b329bee7b5fa.

4. Sophia A. Rosenfeld, *Common Sense* (Cambridge, MA: Harvard University Press, 2011).

5. *Democracy Now!* "Tennessee: Robert Doggart Sentenced to 20 Years over Plot to Massacre Muslims," June 15, 2017, https://www.democracynow.

org/2017/6/15/headlines/tennessee_robert_doggart_sentenced_to_20_years_
over_plot_to_massacre_muslims.

6. Alice Speri, "The FBI Has Quietly Investigated White Supremacist Infiltration of Law Enforcement," *Intercept*, January 31, 2017, https://
theintercept.com/2017/01/31/the-fbi-has-quietly-investigated-white-
supremacist-infiltration-of-law-enforcement.

7. Tara Boyle, Jennifer Schmidt, Rhaina Cohen, Shankar Vedantam, Maggie Penman, and Renee Klahr, "When Is It 'Terrorism'? How the Media Cover
Attacks by Muslim Perpetrators," *NPR*, June 19, 2017, http://www.npr.org/
2017/06/19/532963059/when-is-it-terrorism-how-the-media-covers-attacks-by-
muslim-perpetrators?

8. Dana-Ain Davis, "Narrating the Mute: Racializing and Racism in a Neoliberal Moment," *Souls* 9, no. 4 (2007).

9. Arun Kundnani, *The Muslims Are Coming! Islamophobia, Extremism,
and the Domestic War on Terror* (New York: Verso, 2014), 21.

10. Emma Lazarus, "The New Colossus," 1883.

11. Abdi Ismail Samatar, "Ethiopian Invasion of Somalia, US Warlordism,
and AU Shame," *Review of African Political Economy* 34, no. 111 (March
2007).

12. Jeremy Scahill, "The CIA's Secret Sites in Somalia," *Nation*, December
10, 2014, https://www.thenation.com/article/cias-secret-sites-somalia.

13. Michael Watts, *Silent Violence: Food, Famine, and Peasantry in North-
ern Nigeria* (Atlanta: University of Georgia, 2013).

14. Michael Barbaro, "Debate Heats Up about Mosque Near Ground
Zero," *New York Times*, July 30, 2010, http://www.nytimes.com/2010/07/31/
nyregion/31mosque.html.

15. Robert Schlesinger, "'Ground Zero Mosque' Controversy Shows America's New Nativism," *US News & World Report*, August 11, 2010, https://www.
usnews.com/opinion/articles/2010/08/11/ground-zero-mosque-controversy-
shows-americas-new-nativism.

16. Stephen Sheehi, *Islamophobia: The Ideological Campaign against Muslims* (Atlanta: Clarity Press, 2011), 30.

17. Evelyn Alsultany, "Introduction: Arab Americans and US Racial Forma-
tions," in *Race and Arab Americans before and after 9/11: From Invisible
Citizens to Visible Subjects*, eds. Amaney Jamal and Nadine Naber (Syracuse,
NY: Syracuse University Press, 2006), 1–45.

18. Sunaina Marr Maira, *The 9/11 Generation: Youth, Rights, and Solidarity
in the War on Terror* (New York: New York University Press, 2016), 215.

19. Anny P. Bakalian and Mehdi Bozorgmehr, *Backlash 9/11: Middle Eastern and Muslim Americans Respond* (Berkeley: University of California Press,
2009).

20. Trevor Aaronson, *The Terror Factory: Inside the FBI's Manufactured War on Terrorism* (New York: Ig Publishing, 2014).

21. Matt Apuzzo and Adam Goldman, "The NYPD Division of Un-American Activities," *New York Magazine*, August 25, 2013, http://nymag.com/news/features/nypd-demographics-unit-2013-9/index2.html; Matt Apuzzo and Joseph Goldstein, "New York Drops Unit That Spied on Muslims," *New York Times*, April 15, 2014, https://www.nytimes.com/2014/04/16/nyregion/police-unit-that-spied-on-muslims-is-disbanded.html.

22. Deepa Kumar, *Islamophobia and the Politics of Empire* (Chicago: Haymarket Books, 2012).

23. Pamela Pennock, *The Rise of the Arab American Left: Activists, Allies, and Their Fight against Imperialism and Racism, 1960s–1980s* (Chapel Hill: University of North Carolina Press, 2017).

24. CAIR, "Rep. Peter King's Anti-Muslim Hearings," press release, March 11, 2015, https://www.cair.com/rep-peter-king-s-anti-muslim-hearings.html.

25. Lila Abu-Lughod, *Do Muslim Women Need Saving?* (Cambridge, MA: Harvard University Press, 2013), 30–31.

26. Department of Homeland Security, "If You See Something, Say Something," accessed September 29, 2017, https://www.dhs.gov/see-something-say-something/what-suspicious-activity.

27. Neil Smith, "Deindustrialization and Regionalization: Class Alliance and Class Struggle," *Papers in Regional Science* 54, no. 1 (1984): 113–28.

28. Lydia Saad, "Anti-Muslim Sentiments Fairly Commonplace," Gallup, August 10, 2006, http://news.gallup.com/poll/24073/antimuslim-sentiments-fairly-commonplace.aspx.

29. Philippe Bourgois, *In Search of Respect: Selling Crack in El Barrio* (New York: Cambridge University Press, 2003), 19.

30. Dave Chappelle, *Killing Them Softly*, DVD (Los Angeles: HBO, 2000).

31. George Joseph, "NYPD Officers Accessed Black Lives Matter Activists' Texts, Documents Show," *Guardian*, April 4, 2017, https://www.theguardian.com/us-news/2017/apr/04/nypd-police-black-lives-matter-surveillance-undercover.

32. Betty Medsger, *The Burglary: The Discovery of J. Edgar Hoover's Secret FBI* (New York: Vintage Books, 2014).

33. Betty Medsger, "Just Being Black Was Enough to Get You Spied On by J. Edgar Hoover's FBI," *Nation*, January 22, 2014, https://www.thenation.com/article/just-being-black-was-enough-get-yourself-spied-j-edgar-hoovers-fbi.

34. Apuzzo and Goldman, "NYPD Division of Un-American Activities."

35. Edward Said, *Orientalism* (New York: Vintage, 1978), 42.

36. US Immigrations and Customs Enforcement, "Victims of Crime Engagement Office," accessed September 29, 2017, https://www.ice.gov/voice.

37. Nicholas P. De Genova, "Migrant 'Illegality' and Deportability in Everyday Life," *Annual Review of Anthropology* 31, no.1 (2002).

38. Juan González, *Harvest of Empire: A History of Latinos in America* (New York: Penguin, 2000).

39. Michelle Ye Hee Lee, "Donald Trump's False Comments Connecting Immigrants and Crime," *Washington Post*, July 8, 2015, https://www.washingtonpost.com/news/fact-checker/wp/2015/07/08/donald-trumps-false-comments-connecting-mexican-immigrants-and-crime/?utm_term=.d4f99b5aefc5.

40. Alice Speri, "Top Trump Official John Kelly Ordered ICE to Portray Immigrants as Criminals," *Intercept*, October 16, 2017, https://theintercept.com/2017/10/16/top-trump-official-john-kelly-ordered-ice-to-portray-immigrants-as-criminals-to-justify-raids.

41. Richard Pérez-Peña, "Contrary to Trump's Claims, Immigrants Are Less Likely to Commit Crimes," *New York Times*, January 26, 2017, https://www.nytimes.com/2017/01/26/us/trump-illegal-immigrants-crime.html.

42. Jordan Darville, "Trump Will Publish List of Crimes Committed by Immigrants, in Reflection of Nazi-Era Policy," *Fader*, January 26, 2017, http://www.thefader.com/2017/01/26/trump-crimes-committed-immigrants-nazi.

43. PBS, *First Look: Crossing the Line*, 2012.

44. American Civil Liberties Union, *Abandoned and Abused: Orleans Parish Prisoners in the Wake of Hurricane Katrina*, accessed September 29, 2017, https://www.aclu.org/report/abandoned-and-abused; Michael Patrick Welch, "Hurricane Katrina Was a Nightmare for Inmates in New Orleans," *Vice*, August 29, 2015, https://www.vice.com/en_us/article/5gjdxn/hurricane-katrina-was-a-nightmare-for-inmates-in-new-orleans-829.

45. Barbara Ehrenreich, "Is It Now a Crime to Be Poor?" *New York Times*, August 8, 2009, http://www.nytimes.com/2009/08/09/opinion/09ehrenreich.html.

46. Jeremy Scahill, *Dirty Wars: The World Is a Battlefield* (New York: Nation Books, 2013).

47. American Library Association, "The USA PATRIOT Act," accessed September 29, 2017, http://www.ala.org/advocacy/advleg/federallegislation/theusapatriotact.

48. Sunaina Maira, *The 9/11 Generation: Youth, Rights, and Solidarity in the War on Terror* (New York: New York University Press, 2016), 201.

49. Manning Marable, *Malcolm X: A Life of Reinvention* (New York: Penguin, 2011), 139.

50. Marable, *Malcolm X*, 139.

51. Ryan Devereaux, "Muslim Student Monitored by the NYPD," *Guardian*, February 22, 2012, https://www.theguardian.com/world/2012/feb/22/nypd-surveillance-muslim-student-groups.

52. Begoña Aretxaga, "Terror as Thrill: First Thoughts on the 'War on Terrorism,'" *Anthropological Quarterly* 75, no. 1 (2002): 138–50; Susan Buck-Morss, *Thinking Past Terror: Islamism and Critical Theory on the Left* (New York: Verso, 2003).

53. Gilbert Achcar, *Clash of Barbarisms: The Making of the New World Disorder* (New York: Routledge, 2015), 24.

54. Kumar, *Islamophobia*.

55. Aileen Brown, Will Parrish, and Alice Speri, "Leaked Documents Reveal Counterterrorism Tactics Used at Standing Rock to 'Defeat Pipeline Insurgencies,'" *Intercept*, May 27, 2017, https://theintercept.com/2017/05/27/leaked-documents-reveal-security-firms-counterterrorism-tactics-at-standing-rock-to-defeat-pipeline-insurgencies.

56. Michael Powell, "In Police Training, a Dark Film on U.S. Muslims," *New York Times*, January 23, 2012, http://www.nytimes.com/2012/01/24/nyregion/in-police-training-a-dark-film-on-us-muslims.html.

3. MUSLIM BEAUTY QUEENS AND THE MASTER NARRATIVE

1. The keffiyeh is a traditional Middle Eastern headdress that has come to be a symbol of the Palestinian liberation struggle. In recent decades, the keffiyeh has also become a fashion in the West.

2. Islam in America conference, hosted by the Islamic Center at New York University, February 11, 2012.

3. Negin Farsad and Dean Obeidallah, dirs. *The Muslims Are Coming!* Vaguely Qualified Productions, 2013.

4. Incidentally, Rima Fakih was opposed to the "Ground Zero mosque."

5. Tunku Varadarajan, "Miss USA's Muslim Bikini Diplomacy," *Daily Beast*, May 18, 2010, http://www.thedailybeast.com/miss-usas-muslim-bikini-diplomacy.

6. Ahmed Rehab, "Miss USA Scrutiny Indicates Weird Obsession with Islam," *Huffington Post*, May 25, 2011, http://www.huffingtonpost.com/ahmed-rehab/miss-usa-scrutiny-indicat_b_580995.html.

7. Nida Khan, "The New Miss USA: Progress or Bigger Problems for Muslims?" *Huffington Post*, May 25, 2011, http://www.huffingtonpost.com/nida-khan/the-new-miss-usa-progress_b_585108.html.

8. Ronald Takaki, *A Different Mirror: A History of Multicultural America* (New York: Little, Brown, 1993).

9. Trace William Cowen, "Appalling Video Shows Motorist Harassing 9-Year-Old Girl and Her Mom," *Complex*, June 20, 2017, http://www.complex.com/life/2017/06/video-shows-motorist-harassing-9-year-old-girl-and-mom-fucking-cambodian-nigger.

10. T. P. Fong, *The Contemporary Asian American Experience: Beyond the Model Minority* (London, Pearson, 2002).

11. Ramon Grosfoguel, "The Multiple Faces of Islamophobia," *Islamophobia Studies* 1, no. 1 (2012): 11.

12. Harry Cockburn, "Taj Mahal Remains a Muslim Tomb, Not a Hindu Temple," *Independent*, August 31, 2017, https://www.independent.co.uk/news/world/asia/taj-mahal-hindu-temple-muslim-tomb-india-shah-jahan-wife-bhuvan-vikrama-a7922911.html.

13. Michael E. Miller, "Donald Trump on a Protestor: 'I'd Like to Punch Him in the Face,'" *Washington Post*, February 23, 2016, https://www.washingtonpost.com/news/morning-mix/wp/2016/02/23/donald-trump-on-protester-id-like-to-punch-him-in-the-face/?utm_term=.d9ae10002727.

14. Equal Justice Initiative, "Lynching in America," accessed November 20, 2017, https://lynchinginamerica.eji.org/.

15. *Newsweek*, "The Muslim Moderator," August 18, 2002, http://www.newsweek.com/muslim-moderator-144091.

16. Barack Obama, "Remarks by President at Cairo University, 6-4-09," Obama White House Archives, accessed October 2, 2017, https://obamawhitehouse.archives.gov/the-press-office/remarks-president-cairo-university-6-04-09.

17. Nathan Chapman Lean, *The Islamophobia Industry: How the Right Manufactures Fear of Muslims* (London: Pluto Press, 2012).

18. Mozzochi, "'They Bring That Desert Stuff to Our World': Bill Maher and Islamophobia," *Daily Kos*, November 10, 2014, https://www.dailykos.com/story/2014/11/9/1343681/--They-Bring-That-Desert-Stuff-To-Our-World-Bill-Maher-and-Islamophobia.

19. Edward Said, *Covering Islam: How the Media and the Experts Determine How We See the Rest of the World* (New York: Pantheon, 1981), 55.

20. Olivia Sterns, "Muslim Inventions That Shaped the World," CNN, January 29, 2010, http://www.cnn.com/2010/WORLD/meast/01/29/muslim.inventions/index.html.

21. Stuart Jeffries, "The Muslims Who Shaped America—from Brain Surgeons to Rappers," *Guardian*, December 8, 2015, https://www.theguardian.com/world/2015/dec/08/donald-trump-famous-muslims-us-history.

4. NEOLIBERALISM AND THE GOOD
MUSLIM ARCHETYPE

1. Zareena Grewal, *Islam Is a Foreign Country: American Muslims and the Global Crisis of Authority* (New York: New York University Press, 2013), 302.

2. Moustafa Bayoumi, "The God That Failed: The Neo-Orientalism of Today's Muslim Commentators," in *Islamophobia/Islamophilia: Beyond the Politics of Enemy and Friend*, ed. Andrew Shryock (Indianapolis: Indiana University Press, 2010), 79–93.

3. George W. Bush, "'Islam Is Peace,' Says President," speech delivered September 17, 2011, Washington, DC, transcript, https://georgewbush-whitehouse.archives.gov/news/releases/2001/09/20010917-11.html.

4. *Democracy Now!* "Sudanese Stanford Ph.D. Student Speaks Out," January 30, 2017, https://www.democracynow.org/2017/1/30/sudanese_stanford_phd_student_speaks_out.

5. Sarah Jacobs, "Immigrant Tech Workers in Silicon Valley," *Business Insider*, March 6, 2017, http://www.businessinsider.com/silicon-valley-workers-react-to-trumps-travel-ban-2017-3/#shahrouz-tavakoli-product-designer-pinterest-2.

6. Grewal, *Islam Is a Foreign Country*.

7. Khaled Beydoun, *American Islamophobia: Understanding the Roots and Rise of Fear* (Berkeley: University of California Press, 2018).

8. Hisham Aidi, "Jihadis in the Hood: Race, Urban Islam and the War on Terror," *Middle East Report* 224 (2002): 36.

9. Brennan Center for Justice, "Countering Violent Extremism: A Resource Page," February 12, 2015, https://www.brennancenter.org/analysis/cve-programs-resource-page.

10. Manning Marable, *Beyond Black and White: From Civil Rights to Barack Obama* (New York: Verso, 2016), 189.

11. Will Kymlicka, "Neoliberal Multiculturalism," in *Social Resilience in the Neoliberal Era*, ed. Peter A. Hall and Michèle Lamont (Cambridge: Cambridge University Press, 2013), 99–125.

12. Jodi Melamed, "The Spirit of Neoliberalism from Racial Liberalism to Neoliberal Multiculturalism," *Social Text* 24, no. 4(89) (2006): 8.

13. Keeanga-Yamahtta Taylor, *From #BlackLivesMatter to Black Liberation* (Chicago: Haymarket, 2016).

14. Taylor, *From #BlackLivesMatter*, 103.

15. Deepa Kumar, "Islamophobia: A Bipartisan Project," *Nation*, July 2, 2012, https://www.thenation.com/article/islamophobia-bipartisan-project; Gilbert Achcar, *Clash of Barbarisms: The Making of the New World Disorder* (New York: Routledge, 2015).

16. Ronald Takaki, "The Myth of the Model Minority," in *Sociology: Exploring the Everyday Architecture of Life*, 10th ed., ed. David Newman (Thousand Oaks, CA: Sage, 1995), 255–59.

17. Chimamanda Ngozi Adichie, "The Danger of a Single Story," *TEDGlobal*, July 2009, https://www.ted.com/talks/chimamanda_adichie_the_danger_of_a_single_story.

18. Grewal, *Islam Is a Foreign Country*.

19. Angela Davis, "Gender, Class, and Multiculturalism: Rethinking 'Race' Politics," in *Mapping Multiculturalism*, edited by Avery Gordon and Christopher Newfield (Minneapolis: University of Minnesota Press, 1996), 47.

5. CULTURE TALK AS ISLAMODIVERSION

1. Linda Sarsour, speech, Islamic Society of North America, July 2017.

2. Brian Handwerk, "What Does Jihad Really Mean to Muslims?," *National Geographic News*, October 24, 2003, http://news.nationalgeographic.com/news/2003/10/1023_031023_jihad.html; Abed Awad, "What ISIS—and the West—Gets Wrong about Jihad," CNN, May 29, 2015, http://edition.cnn.com/2015/05/29/opinions/isis-jihad-meaning/index.html.

3. Steven Gregory and Roger Sanjek, *Race* (New Brunswick, NJ: Rutgers University Press, 1994), 9.

4. Walter Rodney, *How Europe Underdeveloped Africa* (London and Dar Es Salaam: Bougle L'Ouverture Publications, 1972); Eduardo Galeano, *Open Veins of Latin America: Five Centuries of the Pillage of a Continent* (New York: New York University Press, 1997).

5. Craig Steven Wilder, *Ebony and Ivy: Race, Slavery, and the Troubled History of America's Universities* (New York: Bloomsbury, 2014).

6. *Real Time with Bill Maher*, "Ben Affleck, Sam Harris, and Bill Maher Debate Radical Islam," HBO, October 3, 2014., https://www.youtube.com/watch?v=vln9D81eO60&t=297s.

7. Salman Rushdie, "Yes, This Is about Islam," *New York Times*, November 2, 2001, http://www.nytimes.com/2001/11/02/opinion/yes-this-is-about-islam.html.

8. Timothy Mitchell, "McJihad: Islam in the US Global Order," *Social Text* 20, no. 4 (2002): 1–2.

9. The exception, for geopolitical and historical reasons, is Iran.

10. An overwhelming majority of these "terrorism experts" focus on religious violence perpetrated by Muslims rather than by non-Muslims.

11. John Nixon, *Debriefing the President: The Interrogation of Saddam Hussein* (New York: Random House, 2017).

12. Department of Homeland Security, "CVE Grants," accessed September 28, 2017, https://www.dhs.gov/cvegrants.

13. Tawfik Hamid, "A Strategic Plan to Defeat Radical Islam," in *Countering Violent Extremism: Scientific Methods and Strategies* (Wright-Patterson Air Force Base, OH: Air Force Research Laboratory, 2015).

14. Stephen Sheehi, *Islamophobia: The Ideological Campaign against Muslims* (Atlanta: Clarity Press, 2011), 32.

15. Michael Prysner, "The Enemy Is the System That Sends Us to War," speech delivered in 2009, transcript on Libcom.org, August 18, 2010, https://libcom.org/library/enemy-system-sends-us-war-speech-iraq-war-veteran.

16. Nazia Kazi, "Voting to Belong: The Inevitability of Systemic Islamophobia," *Identities* (2017).

17. One must wonder whether the teacher *really* thought it was a bomb. If so, bomb-evacuation procedures were not followed. The child was simply arrested and the "bomb" remained, ticking, inside the school.

18. Deepa Kumar, "Islamophobia: A Bipartisan Project," *Nation*, July 12, 2012.

19. Ismat Sarah Mangla, "Hillary Clinton Has an Unfortunate Way of Talking about Muslims," *Quartz*, October 20, 2016, https://qz.com/814438/presidential-debate-hillary-clinton-contributes-to-anti-muslim-bias-in-the-way-she-talks-about-american-muslims.

20. Kumar, "Islamophobia."

6. US EMPIRE'S MUSLIM CHEERLEADERS

1. Muneer Ahmad, "Homeland Insecurities: Racial Violence the Day after September 11," *Social Text* 20, no. 3 (2002): 110.

2. Khizr Khan, speech to the Democratic National Convention, Philadelphia, PA, July 29, 2016, http://www.cnn.com/videos/politics/2016/07/29/dnc-convention-khizr-khan-father-of-us-muslim-soldier-entire-speech-sot.cnn.

3. Michelle Sandhoff, *Service in a Time of Suspicion: Experiences of Muslims Serving in the U.S. Military Post-9/11* (Des Moines: University of Iowa Press, 2017), 4.

4. *Meet the Press*, "Colin Powell Endorses Barack Obama," NBC, October 19, 2008, https://www.youtube.com/watch?v=gs43RR7IiNU.

5. "In Saddam's mind," writes CIA analyst John Nixon, "the two countries were natural allies in the fight against extremism" (see *Debriefing the President: The Interrogation of Saddam Hussein* [New York: Random House, 2017], 2).

6. *Democracy Now!*, "CIA Interrogator Reveals Saddam Hussein Predicted Rise of ISIS," December 28, 2016, https://www.democracynow.org/2016/12/28/part_2_cia_interrogator_reveals_saddam.

7. Mumia Abu-Jamal, "Foreword," in *Islamophobia: The Ideological Campaign against Muslims* by Stephen Sheehi (Atlanta: Clarity Press, 2011), 15.

8. Michael Prysner, "The Enemy Is the System That Sends Us to War," speech delivered in 2009, *LibCom*, August 18, 2010, https://libcom.org/library/enemy-system-sends-us-war-speech-iraq-war-veteran.

9. Sheehi, *Islamophobia*, 59.

10. Michael Barone, "No, It's Not the American Way," *U.S. News & World Report*, May 17, 2004, 40.

11. Arundhati Roy, "Conversation with Howard Zinn," Santa Fe Lensic Performing Arts Center, September 18, 2002, https://lannan.org/images/cf/arundhati-roy-020918-trans-conv.pdf.

12. George W. Bush, press conference, March 21, 2006, https://georgewbush-whitehouse.archives.gov/news/releases/2006/03/20060321-4.html.

13. Tariq Ali, *The Clash of Fundamentalisms: Crusades, Jihads, and Modernity* (New York and London: Verso, 2002), 146.

14. Manning Marable, "9/11: Racism in a Time of Terror," in *Implicating Empire: Globalization and Resistance in the 21st-Century World Order*, eds. Stanley Aronowitz and Heather Gautney (New York: Basic Books, 2003), 1–14.

15. Sheehi, *Islamophobia*, 35.

16. Donald Trump, "Let's get out of Afghanistan," Twitter, January 11, 2013, https://twitter.com/realdonaldtrump/status/289807790178959360?lang=en.

17. Heather Brown, "Ten Years, Over a Trillion Dollars Later: What and How Much Has Changed?" *Jadaliyya*, September 12, 2011, http://www.jadaliyya.com/pages/index/2599/ten-years-over-a-trillion-dollars-later_what-and-h.

18. Chalmers Johnson, *Blowback: The Costs and Consequences of American Empire* (New York: Metropolitan Books, 2000), 7.

19. Johnson, *Blowback*, 65.

20. Junaid Rana, *Terrifying Muslims: Race and Labor in the South Asian Diaspora* (Durham, NC: Duke University Press, 2011), 77.

21. Lesley Gill, *The School of the Americas: Military Training and Political Violence in the Americas* (Durham, NC: Duke University Press, 2004), 4.

22. Aimé Césaire, *Discourse on Colonialism*, trans. by Joan Pinkham (New York: Monthly Review Press, 1972).

23. Enseng Ho, "Empire through Diasporic Eyes: A View from the Other Boat," *Comparative Studies in Society and History* 42, no. 2 (2004): 232–39.

24. Jeremy Scahill, *Blackwater: The Rise of the World's Most Powerful Mercenary Army* (New York: Nation Books, 2007).

25. Johnson, *Blowback*, 7.

26. Jean Bricmont, *Humanitarian Imperialism: Using Human Rights to Sell War* (New York: New York University Press, 2006), 20.

27. Gill, *School of the Americas*, 1.

28. George W. Bush, speech delivered to a joint session of Congress, September 20, 2001, http://www.washingtonpost.com/wp-srv/nation/specials/attacked/transcripts/bushaddress_092001.html.

29. Doug Criss, "Does New Arkansas Law Force Women to Get Rapists' OK Before Getting Abortion?" CNN, July 12, 2017, http://www.cnn.com/2017/07/12/health/arkansas-abortion-law-trnd/index.html.

30. Michelle Alexander, *The New Jim Crow: Mass Incarceration in the Age of Colorblindness* (New York: New Press, 2012).

31. Quoted in Mike Marqusee, *Redemption Song: Muhammad Ali and the Spirit of the Sixties* (New York: Verso, 2005), 214–15.

32. Inderpal Grewal, *Transnational America: Feminisms, Diasporas, Neoliberalisms* (Durham, NC: Duke University Press, 2005); Karen Engle, "Constructing Good Aliens and Good Citizens: Legitimizing the War on Terror(ism)," *University of Colorado Law Review* 75 (2004): 59.

33. Engle, "Constructing Good Aliens," 62.

34. Sheehi, *Islamophobia.*

35. Deepa Kumar, "Islamophobia: A Bipartisan Project," *Nation*, July 2, 2012, https://www.thenation.com/article/islamophobia-bipartisan-project, 195.

36. Arun Kundnani, *The Muslims Are Coming! Islamophobia, Extremism, and the Domestic War on Terror* (New York: Verso, 2014), 16.

37. Corey Robin, "Fear: American Style," in *Implicating Empire: Globalization and Resistance in the 21st Century World Order*, eds. Stanley Aronowitz and Heather Gautney (New York: Basic Books, 2003), 51.

38. Sahar Aziz, "Opening Statement," *Islamic Monthly Debate, CVE*, June 27, 2015, http://theislamicmonthly.com/tim-debate-cve/.

7. BEYOND TRUMP

1. By "establishment Democrat," we mean those Democratic Party leaders who command the most power and control of the party. Establishment Democrats like Joe Biden, Barack Obama, or Hillary Clinton typically work "across the aisle," compromising with and making concessions to the Republican party far more than they work to accommodate the demands of progressives or leftists.

2. Emily Bazelon, "On Abortion, Clinton Takes Ownership of Her Feminism," *New York Times*, October 19, 2016, https://www.nytimes.com/interactive/projects/cp/opinion/clinton-trump-third-debate-election-2016/on-abortion-clinton-takes-ownership-of-her-feminism.

3. Jacob Kushner, "Haiti and the Failed Promise of US Aid," *Guardian*, October 11, 2019, https://www.theguardian.com/world/2019/oct/11/haiti-and-the-failed-promise-of-us-aid.

4. Doug Henwood, *My Turn: Hillary Clinton Targets the Presidency* (New York: Seven Stories Press, 2016).

5. Chris Matyszczyk, "Climate Change, LGBT Rights Removed from White House Website," CNET, January 20, 2017, https://www.cnet.com/news/trumps-white-house-website-removes-climate-change-lgbt-pages/.

6. Samuel Perry, "President Trump and Charlottesville: Uncivil Mourning and White Supremacy." *Journal of Contemporary Rhetoric* 8, nos. 1–2 (2018).

7. Julie Hirschfeld Davis and Maggie Haberman, "Trump Pardons Joe Arpaio, Who Became Face of Crackdown on Illegal Immigration," *New York Times*, August 25, 2017, https://www.nytimes.com/2017/08/25/us/politics/joe-arpaio-trump-pardon-sheriff-arizona.html.

8. Carole McGranahan, "Extreme Speech: A Presidential Archive of Lies: Racism, Twitter, and a History of the Present," *International Journal of Communication* 13 (2019): 19.

9. Rachel Frazin, "New Zealand Suspect Wrote in Manifesto He Supported Trump 'as a Symbol of Renewed White Identity'," *Hill*, March 15, 2019, https://thehill.com/policy/international/434238-new-zealand-suspect-wrote-in-manifesto-he-supported-trump-as-a-symbol-of.

10. David A. Fahrenthold and Joshua Partlow, "5 Questions about President Trump's Use of Undocumented Workers," *Washington Post*, December 4, 2019, https://www.washingtonpost.com/politics/5-questions-about-president-trumps-use-of-undocumented-workers/2019/12/04/29439928-16a2-11ea-a659-7d69641c6ff7_story.html.

11. Todd Miller, "Basically, Donald Trump's Border Wall Already Exists," *Mother Jones*, August 27, 2016, http://www.motherjones.com/politics/2016/08/tomdispatch-operation-streamline-immigration-enforcement-donald-trump-wall/.

12. Tanya Golash-Boza, "2. President Obama's Legacy as 'Deporter in Chief," in *Immigration Policy in the Age of Punishment*, ed. David C. Brotherton and Philip Kretsedemas (New York: Columbia University Press, 2018), 37–56.

13. Peter Borgan and Jennifer Rowland, "Drone Wars," *Washington Quarterly* 36, no. 3 (2013): 7–26.

14. Sheehi, *Islamophobia*, 178.

15. Max Blumenthal, *The Management of Savagery: How America's National Security State Fueled the Rise of Al Qaeda, ISIS, and Donald Trump* (New York: Verso, 2020).

16. Jeremy Scahill, "Blackwater's Youngest Victim," *Democracy Now!*, January 29, 2010, https://www.democracynow.org/2010/1/29/exclusive blackwaters_youngest_victim_father_of_9.

17. Kundnani, *The Muslims Are Coming!*, 7.

18. Tariq Ali, *The Obama Syndrome: Surrender at Home, War Abroad* (New York and London: Verso, 2010), 37–38.

19. Maha Hilal, "Trump Plans to Make It Easier to Kill Civilians with Drones. Sadly, We Can Thank Obama for That," *Foreign Policy in Focus*, October 18, 2017, http://fpif.org/trump-plans-make-easier-kill-civilians-drones-sadly-can-thank-obama/.

20. Ben Norton, "History of US Imperialism in Latin America: From Settler Colonialism to Pink Tide," Moderate Rebels podcast, December 12, 2020, https://moderaterebels.com/history-us-imperialism-latin-america/.

21. Lincoln Blades, "Trump Won by Turning Bigoted Dog Whistles into Megaphones," *Rolling Stone,* May 4, 2016, https://www.rollingstone.com/politics/news/trump-won-by-turning-bigoted-dog-whistles-into-megaphones-20160504.

22. Adam Gabbatt and David Smith, "Trump Accused of Racism after Clash with Asian American Reporter," *Guardian*, May 20, 2020, https://www.theguardian.com/world/2020/may/12/trump-weijia-jiang-china-attack-racism-accusations.

23. Josh Dawsey, "Trump Derides Protections for Immigrants from 'Shithole' Countries," *Washington Post*, January 12, 2018, https://www.washingtonpost.com/politics/trump-attacks-protections-for-immigrants-from-shithole-countries-in-oval-office-meeting/2018/01/11/bfc0725c-f711-11e7-91af-31ac729add94_story.html.

24. Jennifer Hansler, "Breaking with Tradition, Trump White House Forgoes Ramadan Dinner," CNN, June 24, 2017, http://www.cnn.com/2017/06/24/politics/white-house-ramadan-celebration/index.html.

25. Lisa Feldman, Vincent Schiraldi, and Jason Ziedenberg, "Too Little Too Late: President Clinton's Prison Legacy," Justice Policy Institute, February 1, 2001, http://www.justicepolicy.org/research/2061.

26. Luke Savage, "Nancy Pelosi, Which Side Are You On?," *Jacobin,* February 9, 2019, https://www.jacobinmag.com/2019/02/democratic-party-medicare-for-all-pelosi.

27. *Guardian*, "CNN's Van Jones Weeps after Biden's Win: 'It's Easier to Be a Parent This Morning,'" November 7, 2020, https://www.theguardian.com/us-news/2020/nov/07/cnn-van-jones-tears-joe-biden-victory.

28. Rebecca Savransky, "Van Jones: Trump 'Became President' in Moment Honoring Navy SEAL Widow," *Hill*, February 28, 2017, https://thehill.com/homenews/administration/321722-van-jones-on-trumps-honoring-of-widow-of-navy-seal-trump-became.

29. Azeezah Kanji, "Complicity with Imperialism Is Holding Back the Anti-Trump Resistance," *Salon*, December 7, 2019, https://www.salon.com/2019/12/06/complicity-with-imperialism-is-holding-back-the-anti-trump-resistance_partner/.

30. *The Laura Flanders Show*, "Bodies, Borders, Resistance, Rebirth: Arundhati Roy," June 27, 2018, https://lauraflanders.org/2018/06/bodies-borders-resistance-rebirth-arundhati-roy/.

31. Mehdi Hasan, "Mayor Pete Buttigieg on Trump, Islamophobia, and His Presidential Bid," *Intercept*, March 21, 2019, https://theintercept.com/2019/03/21/mayor-pete-buttigieg-on-trump-islamophobia-and-his-presidential-bid/.

32. Sarah Lazare, "Finding the Lesser Evil," *Jacobin*, August 27, 2019, https://jacobinmag.com/2019/08/finding-the-lesser-evil.

33. Sam Levin, "Movement to Defund Police Gains 'Unprecedented' Support across US," *Guardian*, June 4, 2020, https://www.theguardian.com/us-news/2020/jun/04/defund-the-police-us-george-floyd-budgets.

34. Aaron Ross Coleman, "Black Culture Won't Save Kamala Harris," *Nation*, January 28, 2019, https://www.thenation.com/article/archive/black-culture-wont-save-kamala-harris/.

35. Ryan Bort, "DNC Gives Colin Powell More Air Time Than AOC, Millions of Other People Who Didn't Help Start the Iraq War," *Rolling Stone*, August 19, 2020, https://www.rollingstone.com/politics/politics-news/colin-powell-democratic-national-convention-speech-1046493/.

36. Branko Marcetic, "Meet the Hawkish Liberal Think Tank Powering the Kamala Harris Campaign," *In These Times*, October 7, 2019, https://inthesetimes.com/article/center-new-american-security-cnas-kamala-harris-foreign-policy-2020.

37. *Democracy Now!*, "Biden Campaign Attacks Palestinian American Activist Linda Sarsour over Israel Boycott," August 20, 2020, https://www.democracynow.org/2020/8/20/headlines/biden_campaign_attacks_palestinian_american_activist_linda_sarsour_over_israel_boycott.

38. Barack Obama, "Narendra Modi," *Time*, April 15, 2015, https://time.com/3823155/narendra-modi-2015-time-100/.

39. David Brown, "How Women Took Over the Military-Industrial Complex," *Politico*, January 2, 2019, https://www.politico.com/story/2019/01/02/how-women-took-over-the-military-industrial-complex-1049860.

40. Howard Zinn, "Election Madness," *Progressive*, April 8, 2008, https://progressive.org/magazine/election-madness-Zinn/.

41. Timothy Mitchell, "McJihad: Islam in the US Global Order," *Social Text* 20, no. 4 (2002): 1–18.

42. Cornel West and Ben Jealous, "Cornel West & Ben Jealous on Whether Progressives Can Push Joe Biden Leftward If He Defeats Trump," *Democracy Now!*, September 7, 2020, https://www.democracynow.org/2020/9/7/cornel_west_ben_jealous_on_whether.

43. Jamelle Bouie, "The Militarization of the Police," *Slate*, August 13, 2014, http://www.slate.com/articles/news_and_politics/politics/2014/08/police_in_ferguson_military_weapons_threaten_protesters.html.

44. Radley Balko, *Rise of the Warrior Cop: The Militarization of America's Police Forces* (New York: PublicAffairs, 2014).

45. Alice Speri, "Israel Security Forces Are Training American Cops Despite History of Rights Abuses," *Intercept,* September 15, 2017, https://theintercept.com/2017/09/15/police-israel-cops-training-adl-human-rights-abuses-dc-washington/.

46. US Department of Justice, "Investigation of the Chicago Police Department," January 13, 2017, https://www.justice.gov/opa/file/925846/download.

47. James Loewen, *Sundown Towns: A Hidden Dimension of American Racism* (New York: Touchstone, 2005).

48. Michelle Alexander, *The New Jim Crow: Mass Incarceration in the Age of Colorblindness* (New York: New Press, 2012).

49. Alex Emmons, "Commander-in-Chief Donald Trump Will Have Terrifying Powers. Thanks, Obama," *Intercept*, November 11, 2016, https://theintercept.com/2016/11/11/commander-in-chief-donald-trump-will-have-terrifying-powers-thanks-obama/.

8. THE NEVER-ENDING WAR ON TERROR

1. Nicole Nguyen, *A Curriculum of Fear: Homeland Security in US Public Schools* (Minneapolis: University of Minnesota Press, 2006).

2. Henry Giroux, *The University in Chains: Confronting the Military-Industrial-Academic Complex* (Boulder, CO: Paradigm, 2007).

3. George Carlin, *Jammin' in New York* (New York: HBO, 1992).

4. Reuters, "Biden Decides to Stick with Space Force as Branch of U.S. Military," February 3, 2021, https://www.reuters.com/article/us-usa-biden-spaceforce/biden-decides-to-stick-with-space-force-as-branch-of-u-s-military-idUSKBN2A32Z6.

5. Sandra Erwin, "Anti-War Groups Take Aim at Space Force, ICBMs, Missile Defense," *Space News*, November 17, 2020, https://spacenews.com/anti-war-groups-take-aim-at-space-force-icbms-missile-defense/.

6. NFL.com, "The Art of the Flyover," https://www.nfl.com/photos/the-art-of-the-flyover-0ap3000000934319.

7. Katie Lang, "How & Why the DOD Works with Hollywood," US Department of Defense, February 28, 2018, https://www.defense.gov/Explore/Inside-DOD/Blog/Article/2062735/how-why-the-dod-works-with-hollywood/.

8. David Barstow, "Behind TV Analysts, Pentagon's Hidden Hand," *New York Times*, April 20, 2008, https://www.nytimes.com/2008/04/20/us/20generals.html.

9. David Vine, *The United States of War: A Global History of America's Endless Conflicts, from Columbus to the Islamic State* (Oakland: University of California Press, 2020).

10. Donald Shaw and David Moore, "Dems Voting Against Pentagon Cuts Got 3.4x More Money from the Defense Industry," *Sludge*, July 22, 2020, https://readsludge.com/2020/07/22/dems-voting-against-pentagon-cuts-got-3-4x-more-money-from-the-defense-industry/.

11. Gregory Fremont-Barnes, *The Anglo-Afghan Wars 1839–1919* (Oxford: Bloomsbury, 2014).

12. Peter Dale Scott, *The Road to 9/11: Wealth, Empire, and the Future of America* (Berkeley: University of California Press, 2007).

13. Ishaan Tharoor, "The Taliban Indoctrinates Kids with Jihadist Textbooks Paid for by the U.S.," *Washington Post*, December 8, 2014, https://www.washingtonpost.com/news/worldviews/wp/2014/12/08/the-taliban-indoctrinates-kids-with-jihadist-textbooks-paid-for-by-the-u-s/.

14. Ahmed Rashid, *Taliban: Militant Islam, Oil and Fundamentalism in Central Asia* (London: Yale University Press, 2010).

15. Craig Whitlock, "At War with the Truth," *Washington Post*, December 9, 2019, https://www.washingtonpost.com/graphics/2019/investigations/afghanistan-papers/afghanistan-war-confidential-documents/.

16. Gearóid Ó. Tuathail, "'Just Out Looking for a Fight': American Affect and the Invasion of Iraq," *Antipode* 35, no. 5 (2003): 856–870.

17. Jeremy Scahill, "A Brief History of US Intervention in Iraq over the Past Half Century," *Intercept*, April 9, 2018, https://www.youtube.com/watch?v=QYAlSNiFpTc.

18. Donald Rumsfeld, interview by Jamie McIntyre, *CNN Saturday*, September 21, 2002, http://edition.cnn.com/TRANSCRIPTS/0209/21/cst.01.html.

19. Christina Zhao, "Biden Admits Voting for Iraq War 'Was a Mistake,' Says He Did It Because He 'Wanted to Prevent a War,'" *Newsweek*, March 9, 2020, https://www.newsweek.com/biden-admits-voting-iraq-war-was-mistake-says-he-did-it-because-he-wanted-prevent-war-1491369.

20. Andrea Mazzarino, "Indirect Deaths: The Massive and Unseen Costs of America's Post-9/11 Wars at Home and Abroad," *TomDispatch*, January 24, 2021, https://tomdispatch.com/indirect-deaths/.

21. Moustafa Bayoumi, *This Muslim American Life: Dispatches from the War on Terror* (New York: New York University Press, 2015).

22. Mohamedou Ould Slahi and Larry Siems, ed., *Guantanamo Diary* (New York: Little, Brown, 2015).

23. "Museum Store," 9/11 Memorial & Museum, accessed September 25, 2020. https://store.911memorial.org/collections/all-products-on-site.

24. "Memorials," 9/11 Memorial & Museum, accessed September 25, 2020. https://registries.911memorial.org/#/memorials.

25. Peter C. Beller, "Twin Towers, USA," *New York Magazine*, November 18, 2005, https://nymag.com/nymetro/news/people/columns/intelligencer/15157/.

26. Rashid, *Taliban*.

27. Timothy Mitchell, "McJihad: Islam in the US Global Order," *Social Text* 20, no. 4 (2002): 1–18.

28. Steven Salaita, *Inter/Nationalism: Decolonizing Native America and Palestine* (Minneapolis: University of Minnesota Press, 2016).

29. Catherine Lutz, "Making War at Home in the United States: Militarization and the Current Crisis," *American Anthropologist* 104, no. 3 (2002): 723–735.

30. *The Howard Stern Show*, directed by Howard Stern, aired September 11, 2001, on WXRK New York.

31. Chandelis Duster, "Son of 9/11 Victim Criticizes Rep. Omar and 'the Squad' during Speech at Ground Zero," CNN, September 11, 2019, https://www.cnn.com/2019/09/11/politics/september-11-mourner-representative-ilhan-omar/index.html.

32. Sasha Ingber, "'New York Post' Denounced for Publishing Sept. 11 Photo with Rep. Ilhan Omar's Words," NPR, April 12, 2019, https://www.npr.org/2019/04/12/712643034/new-york-post-denounced-for-publishing-sept-11-photo-with-rep-ilhan-omar-words.

33. Joel Westheimer, "Politics and Patriotism in Education," *Phi Delta Kappan* 87, no. 8 (2006): 608–620.

34. Eric Haas and Janice Hart, "Building an Alliance: Empowering Educators through Political Action In and Out of School," paper presented at the National Conference on Empowering Teachers in Times of War, Center for Anti-Oppressive Education, San Francisco, CA, December 6, 2003.

35. Gary Younge, "Silence in Class," *Guardian,* April 4, 2006, https://www.theguardian.com/education/2006/apr/04/internationaleducationnews.highereducation.

36. Westheimer, "Politics and Patriotism."

37. Thea Renda Abu El-Haj, "'I Was Born Here, but My Home, It's Not Here': Educating for Democratic Citizenship in an Era of Transnational Migration and Global Conflict," *Harvard Educational Review* 77, no. 3 (2007): 285–316.

38. Jeremy Stoddard and Diana Hess, "9/11 and the War on Terror in American Secondary Curriculum Fifteen Years Later," in *Reassessing the Social Studies Curriculum: Promoting Critical Civic Engagement in a Politically Polarized, Post-9/11 World*, ed. Wayne Journell (London: Rowman & Littlefield, 2016), 15–28.

39. Cheryl Lynn Duckworth, *9/11 and Collective Memory in US Classrooms: Teaching about Terror* (New York: Routledge, 2014).

40. Andrew Cuomo, "Governor Cuomo Signs Legislation Establishing September 11th Remembrance Day and Moment of Silence at Public Schools," New York State Governor's Press Office, September 9, 2019, https://www.governor.ny.gov/news/governor-cuomo-signs-legislation-establishing-september-11th-remembrance-day-and-moment-silence.

41. Mayida Zaal, "Islamophobia in Classrooms, Media, and Politics," *Journal of Adolescent & Adult Literacy* 55, no. 6 (2012): 555–558.

42. US Department of Education, "911 Materials for Teachers," September 11, 2011, https://www.ed.gov/911anniversary.

43. Stoddard and Hess, "9/11 and the War on Terror," 235.

44. John Nixon, *Debriefing the President: The Interrogation of Saddam Hussein* (New York: Random House, 2017).

45. Mohammad-Mahmoud Ould Mohamedou, *A Theory of ISIS: Political Violence and the Transformation of the Global Order* (New York: Pluto, 2017).

46. George H. W. Bush, "Perspectives/Overheard," *Newsweek*, August 15, 1988, p. 15, archived from the original on December 8, 2015, retrieved October 30, 2015 , https://imgur.com/ieLrziL.

9. CONCLUSION

1. Glenn Beck, *The Glenn Beck Program,* episode aired March 17, 2009. Transcript at https://www.glennbeck.com/content/articles/article/198/22802/.

2. Eric Levitz, "Hillary Clinton Called on Americans to Return to the 'Spirit of 9/12.' Let's Not," *New York Magazine,* June 15, 2016, https://nymag.com/intelligencer/2016/06/clinton-shouldnt-celebrate-the-spirit-of-912.html.

3. *New York Times*, "A Nation Challenged; A Snapshot Gives Bush 90% Approval," September 24, 2001, https://www.nytimes.com/2001/09/24/us/a-nation-challenged-a-snapshot-gives-bush-90-approval.html.

4. CNN, "Britney Spears: 'Trust Our President in Every Decision,'" September 3, 2001. https://www.cnn.com/2003/SHOWBIZ/Music/09/03/cnna.spears/.

5. Sheehi, *Islamophobia*, 64.

6. Corey Robin, "Fear, American Style," *Jacobin*, February 1, 2017, https://www.jacobinmag.com/2017/02/trump-pence-presidency-executive-orders.

7. Nathan Lean, *The Islamophobia Industry: How the Right Manufactures Fear of Muslims* (London: Pluto, 2012); Louise Cainkar, *Homeland Insecurity: The Arab American and Muslim American Experience after 9/11* (New York: Russell Sage Foundation, 2009).

8. *New Arab*, "Economist Paul Krugman Slammed over Tweet Denying Mass Outbreak of Anti-Muslim Sentiment Following 9/11," September 12, 2020, https://english.alaraby.co.uk/english/news/2020/9/12/economist-paul-krugman-slammed-over-tweet-denyingpost-9-11-islamophobia.

9. Blumenthal, *The Management of Savagery*.

10. Robert Jensen, *Citizens of the Empire: The Struggle to Claim Our Humanity* (San Francisco: City Lights Books, 2004), 24.

11. Osama bin Laden, *Messages to the World: The Statements of Osama bin Laden*, trans. James Howarth, ed. Bruce Lawrence (New York: Verso, 2005).

12. Steven Salaita, *Uncivil Rites: Palestine and the Limits of Academic Freedom* (Chicago: Haymarket Books, 2015); David H. Price, *Threatening Anthropology: McCarthyism and the FBI's Surveillance of Activist Anthropologists* (Durham, NC: Duke University Press, 2004).

13. Johanna Bozuwa and Jean Su, "Texas's Energy Crisis Shows Why We Need to Reform Our Privatized Energy System," *Jacobin*, February 24, 2021, https://jacobinmag.com/2021/02/texas-energy-crisis-privatized-system.

14. Chuck Collins, "Updates: Billionaire Wealth, U.S. Job Losses and Pandemic Profiteers," Inequality.org, February 24, 2021, https://inequality.org/great-divide/updates-billionaire-pandemic/.

15. Mike Prysner, "The Real Enemy," speech given in 2009, https://www.youtube.com/watch?v=f07fPAn9KY8. Transcript at https://libcom.org/library/enemy-system-sends-us-war-speech-iraq-war-veteran.

16. Salaita, *Uncivil Rites*, 159.

17. Bayoumi, *This Muslim American Life*, 93.

18. Jensen, *Citizens*, 80.

19. Justice for Muslims Collective, "Abolishing the War on Terror, Building Communities of Care Grassroots Policy Agenda," accessed March 15, 2021. https://www.justiceformuslims.org/grassroots-policy-agenda.

20. Sohail Daulatzai and Junaid Rana, eds., *With Stones in Our Hands: Writings on Muslims, Racism, and Empire* (Minneapolis: University of Minnesota Press, 2018).

BIBLIOGRAPHY

9/11 Memorial & Museum. "Memorials." Accessed September 25, 2020. https://registries. 911memorial.org/#/memorials.

9/11 Memorial & Museum. "Museum Store." Accessed September 25, 2020. https://store. 911memorial.org/collections/all-products-on-site.

Alexander, Michelle. *The New Jim Crow: Mass Incarceration in the Age of Colorblindness.* New York: New Press, 2012.

Ali, Tariq. *The Obama Syndrome: Surrender at Home, War Abroad.* New York: Verso, 2010.

Balko, Radley. *Rise of the Warrior Cop: The Militarization of America's Police Forces.* New York: PublicAffairs, 2014.

Barstow, David. "Behind TV Analysts, Pentagon's Hidden Hand." *New York Times*, April 20, 2008. https://www.nytimes.com/2008/04/20/us/20generals.html.

Bayoumi, Moustafa. *This Muslim American Life: Dispatches from the War on Terror.* New York: New York University Press, 2015.

Bazelon, Emily. "On Abortion, Clinton Takes Ownership of Her Feminism." *New York Times*, October 19, 2016. https://www.nytimes.com/interactive/projects/cp/opinion/ clinton-trump-third-debate-election-2016/on-abortion-clinton-takes-ownership-of-her- feminism.

Beller, Peter C. "Twin Towers, USA." *New York Magazine*, November 18, 2005. https:// nymag.com/nymetro/news/people/columns/intelligencer/15157/.

Bin Laden, Osama. *Messages to the World: The Statements of Osama bin Laden.* Translated by James Howarth. Edited by Bruce Lawrence. New York: Verso, 2005.

Blades, Lincoln. "Trump Won by Turning Bigoted Dog Whistles into Megaphones." *Rolling Stone,* May 4, 2016. https://www.rollingstone.com/politics/news/trump-won-by-turning- bigoted-dog-whistles-into-megaphones-20160504.

Blumenthal, Max. *The Management of Savagery: How America's National Security State Fueled the Rise of Al Qaeda, ISIS, and Donald Trump.* New York: Verso, 2020.

Borgan, Peter, and Jennifer Rowland. "Drone Wars." *Washington Quarterly* 36, no. 3 (2013).

Bort, Ryan. "DNC Gives Colin Powell More Air Time Than AOC, Millions of Other People Who Didn't Help Start the Iraq War." *Rolling Stone,* August 19, 2020. https://www. rollingstone.com/politics/politics-news/colin-powell-democratic-national-convention- speech-1046493/.

Bouie, Jamelle. "The Militarization of the Police." *Slate*, August 13, 2014. http://www.slate. com/articles/news_and_politics/politics/2014/08/police_in_ferguson_military_weapons_ threaten_protesters.html.

Bozuwa, Johanna, and Jean Su. "Texas's Energy Crisis Shows Why We Need to Reform Our Privatized Energy System." *Jacobin*, February 24, 2021. https://jacobinmag.com/2021/02/texas-energy-crisis-privatized-system.

Brown, David. "How Women Took Over the Military-Industrial Complex." *Politico*, January 2, 2019. https://www.politico.com/story/2019/01/02/how-women-took-over-the-military-industrial-complex-1049860.

Bush, George H. W. "Perspectives/Overheard." *Newsweek*, August 15, 1988, p. 15. Archived from the original on December 8, 2015. Retrieved October 30, 2015, https://imgur.com/ieLrziL.

Cainkar, Louise. *Homeland Insecurity: The Arab American and Muslim American Experience After 9/11*. New York: Russell Sage Foundation, 2009.

Carlin, George. *Jammin' in New York*. New York: HBO, 1992.

CNN. "Britney Spears: 'Trust our president in every decision.'" September 3, 2001. https://www.cnn.com/2003/SHOWBIZ/Music/09/03/cnna.spears/.

Coleman, Aaron Ross. "Black Culture Won't Save Kamala Harris." *Nation*, January 28, 2019. https://www.thenation.com/article/archive/black-culture-wont-save-kamala-harris/.

Collins, Chuck. "Updates: Billionaire Wealth, U.S. Job Losses and Pandemic Profiteers." Inequality.org, February 24, 2021. https://inequality.org/great-divide/updates-billionaire-pandemic/.

Cuomo, Andrew. "Governor Cuomo Signs Legislation Establishing September 11th Remembrance Day and Moment of Silence at Public Schools." New·York State Governor's Press Office, September 9, 2019. https://www.governor.ny.gov/news/governor-cuomo-signs-legislation-establishing-september-11th-remembrance-day-and-moment-silence.

Daulatzai, Sohail, and Junaid Rana, eds. *With Stones in Our Hands: Writings on Muslims, Racism, and Empire*. Minneapolis: University of Minnesota Press, 2018.

Davis, Julie Hirschfeld, and Maggie Haberman. "Trump Pardons Joe Arpaio, Who Became Face of Crackdown on Illegal Immigration." *New York Times*, August 25, 2017. https://www.nytimes.com/2017/08/25/us/politics/joe-arpaio-trump-pardon-sheriff-arizona.html.

Dawsey, Josh. "Trump Derides Protections for Immigrants from 'Shithole' Countries." *Washington Post*, January 12, 2018. https://www.washingtonpost.com/politics/trump-attacks-protections-for-immigrants-from-shithole-countries-in-oval-office-meeting/2018/01/11/bfc0725c-f711-11e7-91af-31ac729add94_story.html.

Democracy Now! "Biden Campaign Attacks Palestinian American Activist Linda Sarsour over Israel Boycott." August 20, 2020. https://www.democracynow.org/2020/8/20/headlines/biden_campaign_attacks_palestinian_american_activist_linda_sarsour_over_israel_boycott.

Duckworth, Cheryl Lynn. *9/11 and Collective Memory in US Classrooms: Teaching about Terror*. New York: Routledge, 2014.

Duster, Chandelis. "Son of 9/11 Victim Criticizes Rep. Ilhan Omar and 'the Squad' during Speech at Ground Zero." CNN, September 11, 2019. https://www.cnn.com/2019/09/11/politics/september-11-mourner-representative-ilhan-omar/index.html.

El-Haj, Thea Renda Abu. "'I Was Born Here, but My Home, It's Not Here': Educating for Democratic Citizenship in an Era of Transnational Migration and Global Conflict." *Harvard Educational Review* 77, no. 3 (2007): 285–316.

Emmons, Alex. "Commander-in-Chief Donald Trump Will Have Terrifying Powers. Thanks, Obama." *Intercept*, November 11, 2016. https://theintercept.com/2016/11/11/commander-in-chief-donald-trump-will-have-terrifying-powers-thanks-obama/.

Erwin, Sandra. "Anti-War Groups Take Aim at Space Force, ICBMs, Missile Defense." *Space News*, November 17, 2020. https://spacenews.com/anti-war-groups-take-aim-at-space-force-icbms-missile-defense/.

Fahrenthold, David A., and Joshua Partlow. "5 Questions about·President Trump's Use of Undocumented Workers." *Washington Post*, December 4, 2019. https://www.washingtonpost.com/politics/5-questions-about-president-trumps-use-of-undocumented-workers/2019/12/04/29439928-16a2-11ea-a659-7d69641c6ff7_story.html.

Feldman, Lisa, Vincent Schiraldi, and Jason Ziedenberg. "Too Little Too Late: President Clinton's Prison Legacy." Justice Policy Institute, February 1, 2001. http://www.justicepolicy.org/research/2061.

Frazin, Rachel. "New Zealand Suspect Wrote in Manifesto He Supported Trump 'as a Symbol of Renewed White Identity.'" *Hill*, March 15, 2019. https://thehill.com/policy/international/434238-new-zealand-suspect-wrote-in-manifesto-he-supported-trump-as-a-symbol-of.

Fremont-Barnes, Gregory. *The Anglo-Afghan Wars 1839–1919*. Oxford: Bloomsbury, 2014.

Gabbatt, Adam, and David Smith. "Trump Accused of Racism after Clash with Asian American Reporter." *Guardian,* May 20, 2020. https://www.theguardian.com/world/2020/may/12/trump-weijia-jiang-china-attack-racism-accusations.

Giroux, Henry. *The University in Chains: Confronting the Military-Industrial-Academic Complex.* Boulder: Paradigm, 2007.

Glenn Beck Program, The. Directed by Glenn Beck. Episode aired March 17, 2009. Transcript at https://www.glennbeck.com/content/articles/article/198/22802/.

Golash-Boza, Tanya. "2. President Obama's Legacy as 'Deporter in Chief.'" In *Immigration Policy in the Age of Punishment*, edited by David C. Brotherton and Philip Kretsedemas, 37–56. New York: Columbia University Press, 2018.

Guardian. "CNN's Van Jones Weeps after Biden's Win: 'It's Easier to Be a Parent This Morning.'" November 7, 2020. https://www.theguardian.com/us-news/2020/nov/07/cnn-van-jones-tears-joe-biden-victory.

Haas, Eric, and Janice Hart. "Building an Alliance: Empowering Educators through Political Action In and Out of School." Paper presented at the National Conference on Empowering Teachers in Times of War, Center for Anti-Oppressive Education, San Francisco, CA, December 6, 2003.

Hansler, Jennifer. "Breaking with Tradition, Trump White House Forgoes Ramadan Dinner." CNN, June 24, 2017. http://www.cnn.com/2017/06/24/politics/white-house-ramadan-celebration/index.html.

Hasan, Mehdi. "Mayor Pete Buttigieg on Trump, Islamophobia, and His Presidential Bid." *Intercept*, March 21, 2019. https://theintercept.com/2019/03/21/mayor-pete-buttigieg-on-trump-islamophobia-and-his-presidential-bid/.

Henwood, Doug. *My Turn: Hillary Clinton Targets the Presidency.* New York: Seven Stories Press, 2016.

Hilal, Maha. "Trump Plans to Make It Easier to Kill Civilians with Drones. Sadly, We Can Thank Obama for That." *Foreign Policy in Focus*, October 18, 2017. http://fpif.org/trump-plans-make-easier-kill-civilians-drones-sadly-can-thank-obama/.

Howard Stern Show, The. Directed by Howard Stern. Aired September 11, 2001, on WXRK New York.

Ingber, Sasha. "'New York Post' Denounced for Publishing Sept. 11 Photo with Rep. Ilhan Omar's Words." NPR, April 12, 2019. https://www.npr.org/2019/04/12/712643034/new-york-post-denounced-for-publishing-sept-11-photo-with-rep-ilhan-omar-words.

Jensen, Robert. *Citizens of the Empire: The Struggle to Claim Our Humanity.* San Francisco: City Lights Books, 2004.

Justice for Muslims Collective. "Abolishing the War on Terror, Building Communities of Care Grassroots Policy Agenda." Accessed March 15, 2021. https://www.justiceformuslims.org/grassroots-policy-agenda.

Kanji, Azeezah. "Complicity with Imperialism Is Holding Back the Anti-Trump Resistance." *Salon*, December 7, 2019. https://www.salon.com/2019/12/06/complicity-with-imperialism-is-holding-back-the-anti-trump-resistance_partner/.

Kundnani, Arun. *The Muslims Are Coming!* New York: Verso, 2014.

Kushner, Jacob. "Haiti and the Failed Promise of US Aid." *Guardian*, October 11, 2019. https://www.theguardian.com/world/2019/oct/11/haiti-and-the-failed-promise-of-us-aid.

Lange, Katie. "How & Why the DOD Works with Hollywood." US Department of Defense, February 28, 2018. https://www.defense.gov/Explore/Inside-DOD/Blog/Article/2062735/how-why-the-dod-works-with-hollywood/.

Laura Flanders Show, The. "Bodies, Borders, Resistance, Rebirth: Arundhati Roy." June 27, 2018. https://lauraflanders.org/2018/06/bodies-borders-resistance-rebirth-arundhati-roy/.

Lazare, Sarah. "Finding the Lesser Evil." *Jacobin*, August 27, 2019. https://jacobinmag.com/2019/08/finding-the-lesser-evil.

Lean, Nathan. *The Islamophobia Industry: How the Right Manufactures Fear of Muslims.* London: Pluto, 2012.

Levin, Sam. "Movement to Defund Police Gains 'Unprecedented' Support across US." *Guardian*, June 4, 2020. https://www.theguardian.com/us-news/2020/jun/04/defund-the-police-us-george-floyd-budgets.

Levitz, Eric. "Hillary Clinton Called on Americans to Return to the 'Spirit of 9/12.' Let's Not." *New York Magazine,* June 15, 2016. https://nymag.com/intelligencer/2016/06/clinton-shouldnt-celebrate-the-spirit-of-912.html.

Loewen, James. *Sundown Towns: A Hidden Dimension of American Racism.* New York: Touchstone, 2005.

Lutz, Catherine. "Making War at Home in the United States: Militarization and the Current Crisis." *American Anthropologist* 104, no. 3 (2002): 723–735.

Marcetic, Branko. "Meet the Hawkish Liberal Think Tank Powering the Kamala Harris Campaign." *In These Times,* October 7, 2019. https://inthesetimes.com/article/center-new-american-security-cnas-kamala-harris-foreign-policy-2020.

Matyszczyk, Chris. "Climate Change, LGBT Rights Removed from White House Website." CNET, January 20, 2017. https://www.cnet.com/news/trumps-white-house-website-removes-climate-change-lgbt-pages/.

Mazzarino, Andrea. "Indirect Deaths: The Massive and Unseen Costs of America's Post-9/11 Wars at Home and Abroad." *TomDispatch*, January 24, 2021. https://tomdispatch.com/indirect-deaths/.

McGranahan, Carole. "Extreme Speech: A Presidential Archive of Lies: Racism, Twitter, and a History of the Present." *International Journal of Communication* 13 (2019): 19.

Miller, Todd. "Basically, Donald Trump's Border Wall Already Exists." *Mother Jones,* August 27, 2016. http://www.motherjones.com/politics/2016/08/tomdispatch-operation-streamline-immigration-enforcement-donald-trump-wall/.

Mitchell, Timothy. "McJihad: Islam in the US Global Order." *Social Text* 20, no. 4 (2002): 1–18.

Mohamedou, Mohammad-Mahmoud Ould. *A Theory of ISIS: Political Violence and the Transformation of the Global Order.* New York: Pluto, 2017.

New Arab. "Economist Paul Krugman Slammed over Tweet Denying Mass Outbreak of Anti-Muslim Sentiment Following 9/11." September 12, 2020. https://english.alaraby.co.uk/english/news/2020/9/12/economist-paul-krugman-slammed-over-tweet-denyingpost-9-11-islamophobia.

New York Times. "A Nation Challenged; A Snapshot Gives Bush 90% Approval." September 24, 2001. Reuters. https://www.nytimes.com/2001/09/24/us/a-nation-challenged-a-snapshot-gives-bush-90-approval.html.

NFL.com. "The Art of the Flyover." Accessed March 17, 2021. https://www.nfl.com/photos/the-art-of-the-flyover-0ap3000000934319.

Nguyen, Nicole. *A Curriculum of Fear: Homeland Security in US Public Schools.* Minneapolis: University of Minnesota Press, 2006.

Nixon, John. *Debriefing the President: The Interrogation of Saddam Hussein.* New York: Random House, 2017.

Norton, Ben. "History of US Imperialism in Latin America: From Settler Colonialism to Pink Tide." Moderate Rebels podcast, December 12, 2020. https://moderaterebels.com/history-us-imperialism-latin-america/.

Obama, Barack. "Narendra Modi." *Time*, April 15, 2015. https://time.com/3823155/narendra-modi-2015-time-100/.

Perry, Samuel. "President Trump and Charlottesville: Uncivil Mourning and White Supremacy." *Journal of Contemporary Rhetoric* 8, nos. 1–2 (2018).

Price, David H. *Threatening Anthropology: McCarthyism and the FBI's Surveillance of Activist Anthropologists.* Durham, NC: Duke University Press, 2004.

Prysner, Mike. "The Real Enemy." Speech given in 2009. https://www.youtube.com/watch?v=f07fPAn9KY8. Accessed March 17, 2021. Transcript at https://libcom.org/library/enemy-system-sends-us-war-speech-iraq-war-veteran.

Rashid, Ahmed. *Taliban: Militant Islam, Oil and Fundamentalism in Central Asia.* London: Yale University Press, 2010.

Reuters. "Biden Decides to Stick with Space Force as Branch of U.S. Military." February 3, 2021. https://www.reuters.com/article/us-usa-biden-spaceforce/biden-decides-to-stick-with-space-force-as-branch-of-u-s-military-idUSKBN2A32Z6.

Robin, Corey. "Fear, American Style." *Jacobin,* February 1, 2017. https://www.jacobinmag.com/2017/02/trump-pence-presidency-executive-orders.

Rumsfeld, Donald. Interview by Jamie McIntyre. *CNN Saturday,* September 21, 2002. http://edition.cnn.com/TRANSCRIPTS/0209/21/cst.01.html.

Salaita, Steven. *Inter/Nationalism: Decolonizing Native America and Palestine.* Minneapolis: University of Minnesota Press, 2016.

———. *Uncivil Rites: Palestine and the Limits of Academic Freedom.* Chicago: Haymarket Books, 2015.

Savage, Luke. "Nancy Pelosi, Which Side Are You On?" *Jacobin,* February 9, 2019. https://www.jacobinmag.com/2019/02/democratic-party-medicare-for-all-pelosi.

Savransky, Rebecca. "Van Jones: Trump 'Became President' in Moment Honoring Navy SEAL Widow." *Hill,* February 28, 2017. https://thehill.com/homenews/administration/321722-van-jones-on-trumps-honoring-of-widow-of-navy-seal-trump-became.

Scahill, Jeremy. "A Brief History of US Intervention in Iraq over the Past Half Century." *Intercept,* April 9, 2018. https://www.youtube.com/watch?v=QYAlSNiFpTc.

———. "Blackwater's Youngest Victim." *Democracy Now!,* January 29, 2010. https://www.democracynow.org/2010/1/29/exclusiveblackwaters_youngest_victim_father_of_9.

Scott, Peter Dale. *The Road to 9/11: Wealth, Empire, and the Future of America.* Berkeley: University of California Press, 2007.

Shaw, Donald, and David Moore. "Dems Voting against Pentagon Cuts Got 3.4x More Money from the Defense Industry." *Sludge,* July 22, 2020. https://readsludge.com/2020/07/22/dems-voting-against-pentagon-cuts-got-3-4x-more-money-from-the-defense-industry/.

Sheehi, Stephen. *Islamophobia: The Ideological Campaign against Muslims.* Atlanta: Clarity Press, 2011.

Slahi, Mohamedou Ould. Edited by Larry Siems. *Guantanamo Diary.* New York: Little, Brown, 2015.

Speri, Alice. "Israel Security Forces Are Training American Cops Despite History of Rights Abuses." *Intercept,* September 15, 2017. https://theintercept.com/2017/09/15/police-israel-cops-training-adl-human-rights-abuses-dc-washington/.

Stoddard, Jeremy, and Diana Hess. "9/11 and the War on Terror in American Secondary Curriculum Fifteen Years Later." In *Reassessing the Social Studies Curriculum: Promoting Critical Civic Engagement in a Politically Polarized, Post-9/11 World*, edited by Wayne Journell, 15–28. London: Rowman & Littlefield, 2016.

Tharoor, Ishaan. "The Taliban Indoctrinates Kids with Jihadist Textbooks Paid for by the U.S." *Washington Post,* December 8, 2014. https://www.washingtonpost.com/news/worldviews/wp/2014/12/08/the-taliban-indoctrinates-kids-with-jihadist-textbooks-paid-for-by-the-u-s/.

Tuathail, Gearóid Ó. "'Just Out Looking for a Fight': American Affect and the Invasion of Iraq." *Antipode* 35, no. 5 (2003): 856–870.

US Department of Education. "911 Materials for Teachers." September 11, 2011. https://www.ed.gov/911anniversary.

US Department of Justice. "Investigation of the Chicago Police Department." January 13, 2017. https://www.justice.gov/opa/file/925846/download.

Vine, David. *The United States of War: A Global History of America's Endless Conflicts, from Columbus to the Islamic State.* Oakland: University of California Press, 2020.

West, Cornel, and Ben Jealous. "Cornel West & Ben Jealous on Whether Progressives Can Push Joe Biden Leftward If He Defeats Trump." *Democracy Now!*, September 7, 2020. https://www.democracynow.org/2020/9/7/cornel_west_ben_jealous_on_whether.

Westheimer, Joel. "Politics and Patriotism in Education." *Phi Delta Kappan* 87, no. 8 (2006): 608–620.

Whitlock, Craig. "At War with the Truth." *Washington Post*, December 9, 2019. https://www.washingtonpost.com/graphics/2019/investigations/afghanistan-papers/afghanistan-war-confidential-documents/.

Younge, Gary. "Silence in Class." *Guardian,* April 4, 2006. https://www.theguardian.com/education/2006/apr/04/internationaleducationnews.highereducation.

Zaal, Mayida. "Islamophobia in Classrooms, Media, and Politics." *Journal of Adolescent & Adult Literacy* 55, no. 6 (2012): 555–558.

Zhao, Christina. "Biden Admits Voting for Iraq War 'Was a Mistake,' Says He Did It Because He 'Wanted to Prevent a War.'" *Newsweek*, March 9, 2020. https://www.newsweek.com/biden-admits-voting-iraq-war-was-mistake-says-he-did-it-because-he-wanted-prevent-war-1491369.

Zinn, Howard. "Election Madness. *Progressive*, April 8, 2008. https://progressive.org/magazine/election-madness-Zinn/.

INDEX

9/11 attacks: aftermath, 14–15, 28, 84, 86–88, 112, 115, 117, 121, 122, 123; as justification for war, 83–84, 115, 121; memory of, 126–127; Muslim Americans perceived as responsible for, 18–19, 24, 72; perpetrators, 65; "spirit of 9/12," 92, 125, 126, 127; terminology, 131n2; visual politics and media coverage, 2, 39–40, 125, 126. *See also* Bin Laden, Osama; NSEERS; Patriot Act

Aadam (interviewee), 28
Abu Ghraib prison, 84–85
Abu-Jamal, Mumia, 84
Abu-Lughod, Lila, 28–29, 73
Achcar, Gilbert, 40
Adichie, Chimamanda Ngozi, 66
Affleck, Ben, 72
Afghanistan, 6–7, 28–29, 47–48, 77–78, 86–88, 92, 115, 117, 119, 122, 123, 128. *See also* Bin Laden, Osama; Bush, George W.; Obama, Barack Hussein; Taliban; Trump, Donald; US government
African Americans: Black Lives Matter (BLM), 32–33, 99, 102, 112; civil rights movement, 4, 20–21, 25, 38, 93–94, 100; and dog whistling, 20; Hamza Yusuf on, 50–51; hate crimes against, 100, 125; during Hurricane

Katrina, 40; hypervisibility, 32–33; Jim Crow segregation, 20–21, 48–49, 93–94, 114, 147n48; mass incarceration, 20–21, 92–93, 109, 114, 129; as Muslims, 12, 57, 61; police killings of, ix–x, 109, 112, 114; as politicians, 63–64; protests of Muslim ban, 23–24; under Reagan, 20–21; and slave trade, 12, 71; wealth gap, 20–21. *See also* Black Panther Party; Obama, Barack Hussein; racism; white supremacy
Ahmad, Muneer, 81
Aidi, Hisham, 61
airports: Homeland Security Advisory System ("terror alerts"), 40–41; in India, 47–48; passenger searches, 8–9, 14, 30–31; protests of Muslim ban, 17, 21, 23–24, 24–25, 58, 102; security, 126. *See also* Transportation Security Administration (TSA)
Aisha (interviewee), 38
Alabama bus boycott, 4
Albania, 12–13
Albright, Madeleine, 85–86
Algeria, 50
Ali, Ayaan Hirsi, 95
Ali, Muhammad, 49–50, 93–94
Ali, Tariq, 13, 105, 145n18
Ali, Wajahat, 43, 110
Al-Jazeera, 50